Care Through Touch

Care Through Touch

Massage
as the Art of Anointing

Mary Ann Finch

Continuum　New York

1999

The Continuum Publishing Company
370 Lexington Avenue, New York, NY 10017

Photographs by Cynthia Trenshaw

Printed in the United States of America

Library of Congress Cataloging in Publication Data

Finch, Mary Ann.
    Care through touch : massage as the art of anointing / Mary Ann Finch.
        p. cm.
    Includes bibliographical references.
    ISBN 0-8264-1191-6
1. Massage Miscellanea Handbooks, manuals, etc.   2. Touch—Therapeutic use
Handbooks, manuals, etc.   3. Spiritual healing Handbooks, manuals, etc.   I. Title.
RZ999.F56 1999   99-31312
615.8'22—dc21   CIP

Contents

Acknowledgments

First and foremost I want to acknowledge the men and women who served as models in this book: Lee, Bonnie, Tom, Norma, Martha (Marty), Marc, Dorothy and Anne. I am grateful for their courage to bear witness to the goodness of this work and for their courage to affirm life in the midst of great suffering. Tom and Marc, may you rest in peace!

Next, I offer my deep appreciation to the massage therapists depicted in the pages of this book: Bob Green, Mary Bertrand, Walter Munton, Joanna Walsh, Sabina Henri, Barbara Hill, Jeannie Battagin and Jeff Laevens. They pray their care with skillful hands and loving hearts, making massage a vocation and a profession.

The visual portrayal of this work would not be possible without the generosity, sensitivity and photographic skills of Cynthia Trenshaw, friend and colleague. Her ability to reveal spirituality, as it is being embodied, is a testament to her spiritual life.

This project would never have been possible without the unfailing friendship and encouragement of Jack Miffleton. For the hundreds of hours spent scanning the photos and for laying out and editing this manuscript, I am grateful beyond words.

I owe deep appreciation to five very special people who have helped to fashion the scaffolding of this ministry of caring through touch: Jim O'Hara, administrator of CTI and massage instructor, for his undying support of the "vision"; Jeannie Battagin, my good friend and teaching partner, for her inner beauty, kindness and unfailing dedication to each and every student at CTI; Carol Patron, the Institute's first administrator, whose endless patience and delightful sense of humor kept us on course when there was no course; Pat McLennon, a living prayer and my soul-sister who has assisted in hundreds of Massage: The Art of Anointing Weekends for her gentleness and elegant presence that cloaked each participant with grace; Rich Byrne, my soul friend and brother visionary in the field of embodied spirituality and caring through touch.

Embodied spirituality is about making love incarnate. My deepest gratitude and respect goes to a team of men and women massage therapists who faithfully pour out their compassion and mercy upon the most destitute in San Francisco's Tenderloin District: Don Arel, Jeannie Battagin, Mary Clemency, Dennis Fleming, Bob Green, JoAnn Heinritz, June Keusch, Pat McLennon, Dottie Peterson Joan Prohaska and Cynthia Trenshaw. May you be blessed forever.

I wish to express my gratitude to those Institutes and Pastoral Ministry Programs that welcomed the challenge to embody spirituality in the face of centuries of messages contrary to the sacredness of the body and the healing power of touch: to the Jesuit School of Theology at Berkeley and to the support of two very special friends, James Empereur, S.J., who honored my vision before I had the eyes to see it myself, and to Sandra Schneiders, another sister visionary; to John Mulligan, Clare Ronzani, Cornelius Hubbuck, Don Arel and Dottie Peterson all directors and coordinators of the Institute of Spirituality and Worship. We have always been on the "same page" without ever once having to have a staff meeting. Special thanks too to the School of Applied Theology at Berkeley, to Maureen Terese McGroody, Frank Neihman, Kathleen Gannon and Pat McLennon who tirelessly encouraged the participants to explore the heights and depths of embodied spirituality. Thanks to Tom Gedeon, S.J., past director of Retreats International, a true visionary and the embodiment of love and compassion.

I am very grateful to my publishers at Continuum, especially Eugene Gollogly and Frank Oveis. I knew you understood the intent of this manuscript when you said, "For nearly a decade we have been hearing about embodied spirituality. It is time to embody all those words." Thank you for seeing this as one possible expression.

Last but not least I offer this book and this work of caring through touch as a gift to the marginalized men, women and children who are the forgotten members of society: the homeless, the frail and isolated elderly, the poor, the dying, the mentally ill, the addict. Through you I am leaning the meaning of the sacred teachings of all spiritual traditions: "What you do to the least of my brothers and sisters, you do unto me" (Matthew 25:40). You are my meeting place with God. I honor you now and always.

How to Use This Book

This is a handbook

- for the professional and the non-professional person working with massage.
- for all who wish to incorporate compassionate touch into their ministries, relationships, families and communities.
- for a wide variety of caregivers who want to integrate sacred touch into their pastoral care work in hospitals, extended-care facilities, hospices, AIDS clinics, shelters and drop-in programs for the homeless.

This is a textbook

- for students of massage and massage professionals who wish to explore the spiritual dimensions of massage.
- for students who want to learn about the body as sacrament and the relationship between the sacrament of anointing and the ministry of anointing through massage.
- for students who want to understand the importance of skillful technique combined with respectful and careful personal presence.

This is a source book

- that situates massage in human history and brings the ancient art of anointing with its healing properties into modern ministry and modern care giving.
- that looks to the traditions of both East and West for its inspiration to serve the whole person — body-mind-heart-soul.

This is a reference book

- that provides the necessary information concerning the benefits, precautions and contraindications for using massage in various caregiving situations.
- that provides a basic knowledge of anatomy that will enable the caregiver to massage more intelligently and confidently.

This is a prayer book

- that places massage in the context of Christian care and Gospel values.
- that visually breaks open the meaning of embodied spirituality and incarnational service through the medium of massage and caring through touch.
- that reverences the body, and through the body, honors the human person as sacrament and manifestation of God.
- that transforms massage from a therapy into a blessing.

Introduction

Massage: The Art of Anointing

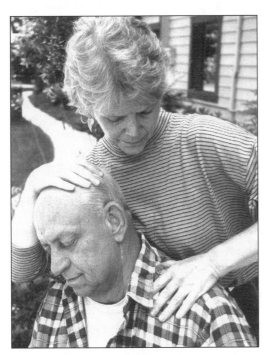

Tom, a physically disabled veteran, is in constant pain. His legs are very swollen despite surgical attempts to patch his arteries. "I don't know how it works," says Tom, " but after a massage I feel so nurtured that I sleep like a baby. When I wake up the swelling is reduced to the point where I can take little walks in the sunshine. I can even do a little volunteer work at the drug counseling center." Tom's doctor says, "Keep the massages coming!"

Sabina is a young mother in treatment for drug addiction. "Massage helps me to be more at peace with myself and my family," says Sabina. In addition to receiving massage, Sabina and other mothers in treatment are taught how to use the soothing power of touch to bond with their children. "I love relating to my children like this," says

Sabina. "It's like I'm learning to bless them instead of beating them."

These stories from the work of the Care Through Touch Institute in Berkeley, California, are just two among hundreds of cases that are heralding the return of massage as a healing art. They attest to the spiritual value of touch in health and healing ministries.

1

Massage as a Ministry

Today, graduates of the Institute work throughout the United States and in other parts of the world successfully incorporating massage into their ministries.

In Guatemala a sister teaches simple massage skills to poor men, women and children living in the barrios. Throughout England and Ireland priests and sisters are offering massage in AIDS clinics, drug-rehabilitation programs and centers for people with learning difficulties. In Germany a school teacher offers massage to poor children in a boarding school. In Chicago's inner city a school counselor provides chair massage to children who have been traumatized by verbal and physical abuse. Our graduates are working as a part of chaplaincy teams in hospitals throughout the United States and Canada. Others are offering their loving services to the elderly and frail in retirement centers, extended care facilities and infirmaries. In an infirmary for religious in Los Angeles, a 94-year-old nun says, "I'll live forever with the kind of treatment my massage therapist is giving me." A missionary priest, teaching religion and philosophy in the Philippines finds time to do massage with blind children and to train other medical students to do the same. In Western Australia one of our graduates provides massage to people receiving grief counselling and also to victims of violence and trauma.

In war-torn central Africa a priest missionary visits a center for handicapped children to bring them comfort through massage. He has trained seminarians and medical personnel to give healing touch. Here is an excerpt from his Christmas letter of 1996:

To my great joy I've been able to practice some massage at the center for handicapped children. I first gave a little face and shoulder massage to the younger ones. They just receive it and smile. The blind, deaf and dumb appreciate the work on the face. They too just smile.

My seminarian friend told me of a conversation between two children: "What is he doing?" asked an older boy to a younger one." I don't know" said the little one, "It's some kind of healing." "What does it do to you?" "It just makes me feel good inside." Later the older boy came up next to me in his wheelchair, his body completely deformed from a muscular disease. He watched, but said nothing. Then I asked, "You want me to help you?" He said , "yes." Now children queue up each time I go. Some just stay close to watch. Well, it's a long and wonderful story. Your work is bearing fruit here.

As I continue to receive reports from our graduates around the world, I am reminded of something Mother Teresa once said:

Love has a hem to her garment

that reaches the very dust.

It sweeps the stains

from the streets and lanes,

and because it can, it must.

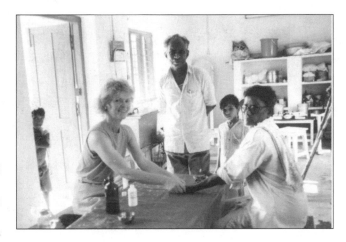

Caring through touch, caring as Jesus cared, is more than an optional service for the poor, it is their nourishment. Would that it were their "daily bread!"

Our approach to massage has given sexually and physically abused women and men a healthy, respectful and non-abusive experience of touch. We have provided regular massage to people who live every day with chronic pain, and to those with life threatening diseases. We are returning massage to hospitals: rubbing the hands and feet, soothing the necks, shoulders and backs of patients, staff, and family members. Our volunteers are taking massage to homeless shelters to offer the gift of a few minutes of care, respect and tenderness. Massage in this context is part of an embodied spirituality, attentive to the wisdom of a body in pain. It is at home wherever humans are living, suffering and dying.

Often as people begin to trust, to relax, and to accept skilled touch, they will begin to talk, unwinding the threads of their life stories. These are vulnerable moments, and the gift of skilled hands assures them that whatever their stories, in this ritual they are accepted unconditionally. Sometimes the comforting touch of massage will be the last touch they know before going to sleep. A homeless woman in an Oakland shelter said to me, "You can't imagine what this back massage means after a day full of rejections."

Through skilled touch our Institute strives to bring a sense of wholeness and beauty to human beings who find themselves in the midst of chaos, sickness, violence and ugliness. We teach the skills of massage that can be adapted to all kinds of conditions and circumstances. The philosophy of the Institute and its training is simply *care* — **care through touch.**

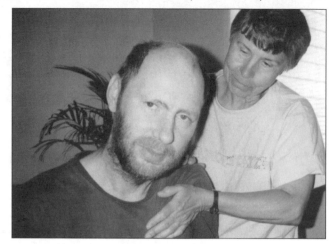

Massage as an Art

This manual medicine called "massage" is the oldest known healing art. Our ancient tribal parents cared for their children, the sick and the elders by rubbing their bodies with oil and spices. Apart from its curative qualities, massage was a sign, in ritual, of respect and love. It helped create a closeness and communication within the tribe that was necessary for survival as a community.

Massage has been practiced in Europe since the time of Hippocrates (480 B.C.). The early physicians Celsus and Galen broadly applied massage as a remedy for relieving pain. In the *Odyssey*, Homer describes the restorative qualities of massage for exhausted war-worn soldiers. From its origins massage was unique in its ability to restore and maintain health and to communicate loving care between humans.

In the East, massage as a medical therapy has always been part of a healing tradition that values the connection of the mind, body and spirit. Eastern physicians were practicing massage at least 3000 years before the birth of Christ. In one of the oldest medical texts, the *Nei Ching,* massage is named as one of the basic medical treatments.[1]

In writings from ancient India, Egypt, Persia and Japan there are many references to the benefits of massage. Today in the East it is an integral part of family life as well as a skilled therapy.[2]

In India I witnessed the beautiful ritual of anointing a newborn baby. Within seconds after the cutting of the umbilical cord, the mid-wife placed the tiny baby face down upon the bare legs of the grandmother, sitting on the ground. First, she bathed the infant; then, using olive oil she rubbed the baby in confident, knowing ways. Repeatedly, she turned him and stroked him with her hands; she stroked him with her eyes and her heart. Her anointing touch was loving, sensitive and responsive to the slightest quiver or whimper from this new being. She was indeed a priestess, performing a sacred art — an art of welcoming and caring through touch!

This ritual of love has been a part of India's heritage for thousands of years. By nurturing the child through this ritual an easy non-verbal communication between infant and parents begins from the very first days of life. Today, the International Association of Infant Massage, founded by Vimala McClure in 1976, preserves this tradition and teaches parents and health care professionals worldwide the theory and art of infant massage.

The practice of massage remained relevant in the West until the Middle Ages when the physical body came to be seen largely as an enemy of the spirit, and the pleasures of the flesh were either suppressed or held in contempt. Christianity's overemphasis on afterlife, preparing the soul for death, and denial of the body needlessly pitted the soul against the body.

The Renaissance and the Enlightenment brought renewed interest in the body and physical health. Leading physicians incorporated massage into their therapies.

treating the kings of France with massage therapy.

Many present-day massage techniques began in the early nineteenth century with Swedish gymnast and fencing master, Per Henrick Ling. During travels in China, Ling acquired massage skills and then combined these techniques with his knowledge of gymnastics and anatomy. From this synthesis came what is still known today as Swedish Massage.

In recent years massage came to the forefront through the human potential and personal growth movements of the 1960's and 70's. At the Esalen Institute in Big Sur, California, massage became a powerful therapeutic tool that was explored in a wholistic and spiritual way. Today the fields of medicine, psychology and pastoral ministry are rediscovering the value of massage and touch therapies. Membership in the American Massage Therapy Association has grown steadily, reflecting the renaissance of massage as a respectable and effective form of health care.

Today in *Massage: The Art of Anointing*, the best of the modern massage techniques combine with the ancient spiritual healing, symbolized in human hands, to bring comfort and care to the sick and infirm. In *Massage: The Art of Anointing* the ministry of hands and anointing touch are human ways for Christians to embody the Christ of the New Testament, the Divine Healer.

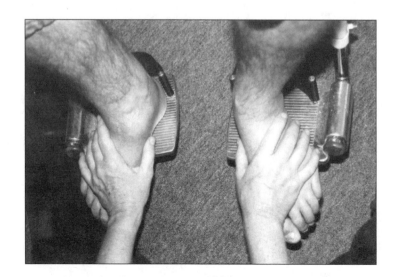

Massage as Anointing

As a Christian, a teacher and a professional massage therapist, I look at massage as the art of anointing, as a sacrament of touch, for it links one of the oldest and simplest of medical treatments with the ancient powers of "the laying on of hands" and the "anointing with oil." Hands are symbols of human service, and communicators of the healing potential within. Oil is a biblical symbol of the divine gift of health, strength and respect for the whole person. In massage these symbols coalesce to comfort and strengthen the whole being.

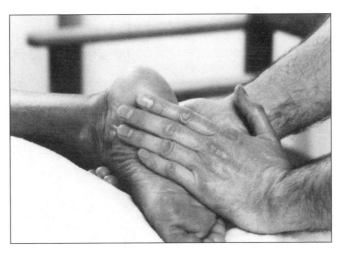

Babu is a person living with leprosy in South India. I met him and many other lepers while volunteering as a massage therapist in the "colony" they call home. Late one night I heard screaming coming from the clinic. It was not the cry of childbirth I had often heard there. This was a man's painful cries. I hurried to the clinic. It was Babu. He and a few other men had gone into town to beg. On the way home he was attacked, badly beaten and robbed by several young marauders. The beating had opened his leprous sores, and the wagon ride back to the colony over the rutted dirt road had added to his agony.

While the doctor unbandaged his feet and began to sterilize his wounds, I washed my hands, donned a mask, gown and gloves. I poured a few drops of heavy medicinal olive oil into my hands. I moved up along side the table and placed my hand on his heaving chest. The stench from his sores was acrid. He screamed with each touch of the doctor's probe, but I continued to lay my hand on him and brought all of my attention and intention to be with him and care for him in the way I knew best.

Suddenly he flung his arm across his chest and gripped my hand and began rub-

bing my hand. It was a special moment, a moment of relationship. He stopped crying, and I stopped noticing the horrible smell. For a suspended time, we connected in a way possible only through touch. I was alone and miles from home; Babu was clinging to life, but for that moment neither of us was alone or afraid. Babu survived that night.

The next morning when I went into the men's ward in the clinic, Babu was sound asleep. Softly I placed my hand on his chest . Babu slept on, but something inside my body was wide awake and listening. "If we do not know the gospel in our bodies." writes James Nelson, " we do not know the gospel." [3] For this moment, I knew the gospel. I heard it in my body. I knew Babu's leprous body was a hospice for the holy, and my silent presence through touch was a prayer.

The physiological and psychological effects of massage are well known, but massage as the art of anointing is an experience of touch that opens up possibilities for healing on the spiritual level as well. In its sacramental dimension massage reaches and soothes deep wounds, memories and fears by releasing the healer, "the Anointed One," within. As such, massage is a prayer and a celebration of the body as a sacrament, a temple of God's life.

Massage as Prayer

In the healing ministry of massage, our hands are visible prayers. When we take the time to bring the palms of our hands together attentively in the reverent gesture of wholeness and holiness, and hold them before our hearts, the life inside us and the sacred spirit within the hands wakes up and takes notice. I usually begin and end each massage by placing my hands together in this way and bowing to myself and to the person I am with. I do not see this as a pious gesture, but a prayerful reminder of my ministry. This same gesture in the Hindu and Buddhist tradition is one of deep respect for the whole person. This gesture of the praying hands announces the sacramental and compassionate nature of the touch even before the massaging actually begins. It anoints and affirms the goodness of the human body and blesses the environment for what is to happen here. In all my years of doing this work, never once has anyone ever asked me what I was doing when I made my bows. Somehow or other, they always know. The gesture is subtle, like a whiff of incense. Sometimes the receiver sighs almost in relief at that moment, a quiet surrender to the healing power of unconditional care.

In my twenty years of practicing as a massage therapist, and of passing on the "art of anointing" as a teacher of massage, I have yet to meet a pair of hands that did not qualify for the job.

It was on Holy Thursday that all of the staff and volunteer-interns from our school in Berkeley went together to a low-income housing project in Oakland to provide chair massages to the residents, all of whom have serious physical disabilities. Before coming to live here, many of these men and women had spent some years of their life in prison, or on the streets. They have known the ravages of poverty, drugs, crime, and sexual abuse. Some are tough and gruff; others are weak and emaciated from AIDS; still others are disabled from an assortment of injuries, accidents and diseases. For the most part, they are feared and shunned by society.

Since our interns go here weekly to provide massage for as many of the residents as possible, they are almost like the Institute's extended family. About a week before the community chair massage took place, I had sent a letter to all the residents in the house, suggesting that after the massage therapist finished giving them a chair massage, they might want to give back the gift of touch, and I suggested that they might do a hand massage for their therapist. What happened was touching and sacramental.

At first there were the natural signs of embarrassment and hesitancy, but then they each settled into their own unique rhythms. I saw gnarled and arthritic hands, large callused hands, trembling hands, small hands and long elegant hands, each uniquely signing love. We saw hands that had once known violence become gentle and composed. We saw hands transformed from ordinary flesh into sacred vessels of mercy and care. It was a holy moment — a holy Thursday, and for those of us familiar with the traditional foot washing rituals of Holy Thursday, this was the Good News alive and surfacing again in unexpected ways.

This one prayerful experience opened the door to a weekly training program in Care Through Touch at this residential site. A small group of residents are now learning safe and simple ways of touching, comforting and connecting with their neighbors and friends, and in doing so they are healing their own wounds of isolation and resentment.

Ministers of massage can take as a charter the words of Isaiah that Jesus read in beginning his ministry:

> *The Spirit of the Lord is on me, because he*
>
> *has anointed me to preach*
>
> *good news to the poor.*
>
> *He has sent me to proclaim freedom for the*
>
> *prisoners and recovery of sight for the blind,*
>
> *to release the oppressed.* (Luke 4:18)

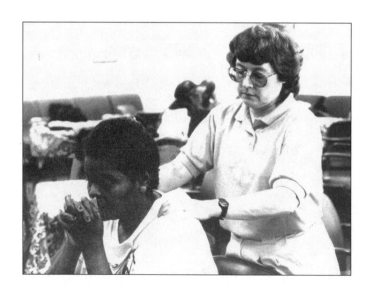

Massage as Compassion

If massage is an act of prayer it is also an act of compassion. By compassion, I mean "the desire to be present to and receive the suffering of another." Compassion becomes an art when an action, such as massage, informs our way of being with another person, especially when that person is experiencing painful or vulnerable moments. Often I have settled the warm palm of my hand over a frightful looking scar and silently been with the person as they descended into the darkened tomb of that wound in search of its healing power. Repeatedly, I am *amazed* that the most wondrous of all the massage strokes is that of the "laying on of hands," of simply resting my hands, my intentions, my heart in the other as one would rest in contemplative prayer.

A few years ago, while volunteering at Mother Teresa's Home for Dying Destitutes in Calcutta, I was assisting one of the male nurses in dressing the wounds of a man whose skin appeared to be pasted over his bones. He moaned as the bandages were removed from his shoulder and hip. I was shocked to see how rats had gnawed away large sections of skin and muscle tissue. The nurse tenderly cleaned and dressed the wounds. The man grimaced in pain. I crouched down on the opposite side of the litter and took his hand in mine, gently massaging it. Slowly he turned his face from the nurse to me. His eyes, reflecting deep pools of suffering engulfed me and drew me in. We held one another with eyes and hand. He received my poor efforts to care, and I received his trust and gratefulness. Caring through touch required very little effort here.

Compassionate massage is embodied contemplation. A silent caring touch for a fellow human at the end of his journey becomes a prayerful anointing.

As ministers and givers of care, we have endless opportunities every day to care for others by touching their suffering. Some of us may feel so inadequate doing this that we may literally quake every time we step across the threshold of another person's pain. Others might put on the gloves of professional degrees and begin talking; still others of us may pronounce the holy words and perform the holy rites.

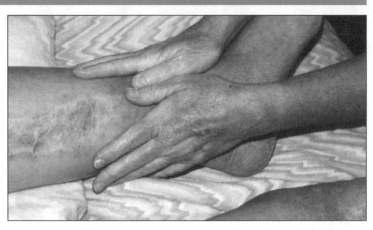

There is no one right way. But if we are graced enough to trust ourselves, we can bring an anointing touch to someone in need. When our hands are skillful, guileless and Christ-like, compassion and contemplation will join the ancient art of massage.

Benefits a Hundredfold

The benefits of a skilled touch, as in massage, are endless. Massage brings about a welcome release of tension throughout the body. The various pressures and rhythmic dance-like movements of the massage strokes help to eliminate toxic deposits; massage stimulates nerve endings, making the receiver and giver alike much more responsive to the touch of the surrounding environment; it improves muscle tone by stretching the muscles, opening the joints and facilitating a greater capacity for movement; it stimulates both the circulatory and immune systems, enabling them to move more effectively the fluids that carry waste products from and nourishment to all parts of the body. Massage benefits the functioning of the heart, normalizing the heart-rate; it helps one breathe more naturally and efficiently and digest more effectively. Many studies validate the importance of relaxation for the healing of the whole person.

Pregnant Women

Massage during pregnancy helps to relieve some of the unhealthy side effects of physical and psychological stress during this time as well as during labor and delivery. Various forms of touching, especially rocking, stroking, rubbing and holding do wonders to reduce the discomfort, soothe the fears, and manage some of the fatigue that are all a part of this stressful time. In the hours preceding birth, Massage, The Art of Anointing can be as simple as holding the mother's hand or putting a firm arm around her waist while she's walking; or supporting her through a contraction by stroking her head and face, or rubbing her shoulders and her back. These acts of care can be given by a massage therapist, a friend, a partner, even a child in the case of a home birth. In the majority of cases, fathers and other family members love sharing in the birth of their child or their sibling in these ways. Because of the intimate nature of touch, it gives the parents and family a chance to stay in touch with each other at this critical and miraculous time.

Infants

Massage throughout pregnancy, labor and delivery is a natural prelude to baby massage. Touch has been called the "mother sense" because it is the very first of all the senses to develop *in utero*. Dr. Tiffany Field, director of the Touch Research

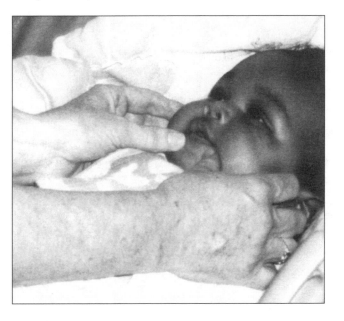

Institute and professor of psychology at the University of Miami Medical School in Miami, Florida, has been conducting and documenting the benefits of massage to infants for over a decade. While her studies have focused to a great extent on premature and drug-exposed babies, the results can be generalized to include well babies also. Infants receiving massage during the first days of life gain weight and develop almost twice as fast as infants who are not being massaged; they leave the hospital sooner and the over-all costs of health care are significantly reduced. Today, Dr. Field's work is being acknowledged by health-care professionals all over the world.

In Hospitals

California Pacific Medical Center in San Francisco is one of the largest private not-for-profit patient care, education and research centers on the west coast. In 1985, this hospital introduced massage therapy as an important humanistic complement to the high-tech health-care environment. The Massage Therapy Vision Statement for the Medical Center reads:

Massage therapy nurtures the body and spirit through safe, compassionate touch, validating self-worth, enabling the individual to focus on their own well-being and extending the concept of healing beyond high-tech care.

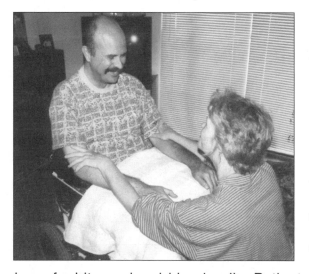

The benefits to the patients have been impressive. Recovery is accelerated when muscular tension, soreness, fatigue, anxiety and pain are lessened. Massage helps the body to eliminate the toxins and waste products that build up rapidly when physical movement is restricted and medical interventions are constant and intense. Definite changes in blood chemistry have been observed, including an increase in the number of white and red blood cells. Patients also notice that following a massage they sleep better, they experience less pain, or are better able to tolerate pain, and therefore request less pain medication; they feel less anxious and more positive about the hospital environment.

"It's wonderful," says Tedi Dunn, founder of the hospital's Massage Therapy Service, "to be able to offer something pleasant and comforting when so much of a patient's day involves enduring pain, tests, IV sticks and blood draws." [4]

The Seriously Ill

Massage for people with AIDS/HIV is a healing and satisfying experience for both giver and receiver. Service Through Touch, a non-profit organization founded and directed by Irene Smith, was one of the very first attempts to create a community of volunteers that would provide skilled and compassionate touch to people with AIDS and other life-threatening diseases in San Francisco. Since 1983, this service has spread from San Francisco throughout the world. Today, it provides international trainings for health-care professionals, massage volunteers, family and friends, to further their knowledge of touch and massage in critical care situations.

It is a very moving experience to touch someone who is touch-deprived or who, because of AIDS, is shunned by society. These human beings are the modern-day lepers, and a caring touch can be deeply reassuring and nurturing. In many of the places our therapists and interns work, people are nearing the final stages of life due to this disease. Often they are too weak to talk, but their eyes and their skin can speak: "Yes. Please touch me; let me know that you care about me." With our eyes, and our hands we can reach out to them with the tenderness of a mother, a father and a friend, saying, "Yes, I do care about you!"

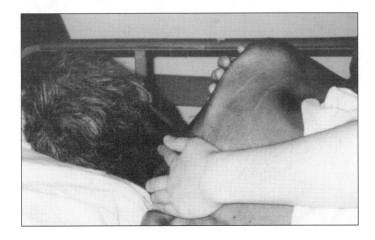

The Elderly

Tactile needs do not seem to change with aging .

. . . It is especially in the aging that we see touching at its best, as an act of spiritual grace and a continuing human sacrament. [5]

Across the country many nursing homes, extended-care facilities and retirement communities are beginning to use massage and care through touch as a regular component of their patient management. The benefits of massage for the elderly parallel those for people with serious illnesses and for those in hospital settings. Massage enhances blood and lymph circulation, stimulates the nervous system, softens tense, tight muscles and enhances the functioning of the digestive and respiratory processes. These effects are especially beneficial to older people who, due chiefly to the aging process, will experience more circulation problems, stiffness and pain in the joints. Touch is a natural and therapeutic way of being with the elderly. It is relaxing and healing, and at the same time pleasurable and sacred. Touch and its life-enhancing benefits are too frequently denied the elderly in our culture. Often they are alone in the world, and the only kind of physical contact they may still experience comes to them in the form of brief medical attention.

Massaging an elderly person with a healing intent rather than probing for a "condition" helps to bring good feelings about themselves and their bodies. I remember massaging both my mother and my father in the last stages of their lives. They were like innocent children in my arms.

Father Michael is an old friend and former colleague, a priest who now has Alzheimer's disease. He was once a charismatic preacher with a robust body and equally robust heart. I had not seen him for a few years, and heard that the disease had stolen his old spirit, and that his speech was halting and incoherent.

I arrived at the nursing home in the late afternoon. I pushed open his door a crack and looked in. He was taking a nap. I tiptoed in and sat down on the side of his bed. I reached out and began slowly and softly to rub his neck and back. Then, as if he were a child pretending to sleep, he opened his eyes. To my surprise he recognized me and called me by my name. "Mary Ann," he said, "I can't believe you came all this way to see me."

I continued to massage his arm and hand as we talked. For some reason I started humming "Amazing Grace." Michael joined right in, remembering every word. He loved to sing and was proud that he could always be heard above the congregation. For these few moments through touch he was the old Michael, and I saw that robust heart again.

In our Institute's outreach work we often encounter elderly men and women with Alzheimer's disease. It is easy, as a caregiver or family member, to become overwhelmed by the confusion these people live with much of the time. As I found with Fr. Mike, sometimes something as little as holding or stroking a hand can awaken them, and for a few moments bring them back to the here and now. "The right kind of touch given at just the right moment, can cut through the delusions of the mind like a sword through butter." [6]

Obstacles to Massage — Befriending the Body

"I have never liked my body," a 47-year-old woman said to me sadly, "I've avoided being in it almost all my life. For the most part, my body has given me nothing but trouble in the past 20 years. Why should I love it? I've had two heart attacks and now breast cancer. I've already had a mastectomy on one breast, and I feel that my body isn't pretty anymore. I'd be embarrassed for anyone to see my body, much less touch

me. I don't even want to touch myself. I half-close my eyes and hold my breath when I'm bathing, or dressing and undressing. When I talk about it like this, my body feels like it wants to cry. I feel like I want to cry. "

For reasons of religion, culture or parenting many of us grew up believing that our bodies were undependable, that they could get sick, injured and let us down. We were rarely given permission to love our bodies or to take satisfaction in the joy to be had through them. Perhaps we were cautioned against touching our bodies. How often after infancy were we held in healthy loving ways? Many of my male clients rarely remember an embrace from their fathers.

The greatest obstacles to embracing massage as a ministry are unhealthy attitudes, beliefs and feelings about our bodies. Healthy training in the ministry of massage provides a safe and honest environment in which to communicate with the body and its history and to speak and share frankly about bodily feelings.

In the last two decades the body has enjoyed the spotlight in the vast commercialization of physical fitness with its attending products which promise the virtual correction of all the Creator's mistakes! Exercise and fitness programs have become a part of the everyday life of millions of people. The parks are filled with joggers; memberships at health clubs are at an all-time high; corporations are encouraging their employees to participate in stress management classes; some businesses have built their own fitness centers and allow employees to use the facilities on company time. Other corporations employ on-site massage therapists to provide l0-l5 minute chair massages as a stress reduction measure. Retirement centers advertise programs in fitness and nutrition; people practicing yoga and T'ai chi ch-uan can be seen along beaches and in public parks; body therapies, such as massage, movement, Rosen bodywork, acupressure, meditation practices, not long ago considered suspect and self-indulgent, are now regularly prescribed by physicians, psychotherapists and spiritual directors. Almost every bookstore stocks a health and spirituality section with the latest magazines, books and videos on nutrition, exercise, massage, beauty tips, relaxation and meditation.

This current interest (if not compulsion) in health, generic spirituality and fitness reveals, on the one hand, a genuine desire to experience all dimensions of the life of the body as one's own. On the other, it is so intent on producing results that conform to cultural ideas of health and beauty and holiness that the real learning may be missed. It is, in fact, the fitness industry that helps perpetuate the tyranny of thinness, the hard body and the flat stomach. The cry of the spirit may be difficult to hear amid the clamor of the Nautilus machines, the rattle of the weights and the pounding of the aerobic beat.

Massage and body work are wholistic when they allow information from deep within to come forth. Rather than beating the body into submission to current trends, in wholistics we honor the body as a holy temple. We condition the body through massage, exercise, proper diet, rest, relaxation and meditation in ways that allow self-learning and self-discipline to occur. The process itself is what is important in wholistic spirituality, not the possible end result. It is in the journey that one finds and feels the integration of body and spirit.

One does not reach wholeness by receiving a diploma at the successful completion of a fitness or massage program. One achieves wholeness in the daily awareness of oneself as body, in the fits and groans that bring the spirit to birth from the skeletal and organic depths of one's self.

In a wholistic spirituality we celebrate not the body beautiful but the body sacramental. This approach finds the locus of God's presence in the very bodiliness and sensuality of each human being, and celebrates the body as a sacrament of God's life, a sign of ongoing creation and unity with Christ and all who make up Christ's body.

The Body as a Manifestation of the Spirit

Maurice Leenhardt, longtime missionary to the Canakas of New Caledonia, once suggested to a native convert that what Christianity had brought to the Canaka world view was the idea of spirit. The convert replied that this was not at all the case. What Christianity had added was the notion of body, for prior to Christianity the Canakas did not really think of themselves as distinct persons, but this new notion of body gave them a way of seeing one another as individuals and of experiencing personhood. [7]

That Christianity can be more a revelation of the body than of the spirit may be surprising to many Christians baptized in Cartesian and Pauline waters, where the mind is clearly superior, where bodily experiences and spiritual quests are often seen at war on ancient battlefields, and where victory over the body is what finally leads to religious freedom. While this attitude is still very much alive, let us not dwell on the many forms of religious hostility to the body, but consider the many hopeful signs for Christians today in reclaiming the body as a manifestation of the spirit. As the humanity of Christ is a sacrament of our unity with God, so our own humanity, our bodily way of being in the world can be a source of spiritual knowledge, a guide on our quest, the very ground of our being and a new Bethlehem where the word continues to be enfleshed.[8]

"There is no salvation apart from the body," writes Dr. John Mabry.[9] For Christians, the mystery of Christ's Incarnation is a central event in God's creation and care for all. But the incarnation of God is not confined to Jesus Christ. The embodiment of God, not just in Jesus of Nazareth, but in every living being, is at the heart of the Christian experience and embodied spirituality. The presence of Christ as a human being  is nothing less than God's resounding incarnation in all human life. Contrary to the dualism we find in teachings that place the soul at war with the body, the more wholesome spiritual traditions view the world and the human body as a blessing, a noble thing. Norman Brown suggests that "The last thing to be realized is the incarnation. The last mystery to be unveiled is the union of humanity and divinity in the body."[10]

At Home with Your Body

No doubt you can remember times when you felt completely at home with your body. Perhaps it was running along a beach with your body wrapped in wind and mist; dancing with abandon; leaping to your feet after a performance that stirred you deeply; or running into the waiting arms of a friend. These are moments of pulse and vigor, moments where flesh and spirit find integration. These can be sacred moments where you are acutely aware of your sensual connection to the Creator, and creation.

If we are surprised that our very bodiliness can lead us to such liminality, carrying us across sacred thresholds, if these moments are rare and infrequent, then perhaps we do not see the body as friend and guide, perhaps we do not consider our own incarnation as the centerpiece and hearth of human living. The simple fact is that our own bodies hold the secret of who we are. By becoming more fluent in the language of the body we can learn to relate more honestly and responsibly to ourselves and to the feelings of others.

Every day in my work as a body-based counselor and spiritual director, I encounter people who assault, reject and punish their bodies. They work relentlessly, neglecting nutrition and exercise. Like so many others they take their bodies for granted until they are beset by some illness, physical or psychological, and then often look for a quick fix. Even among many who exercise regularly the mind/body connection can go unnoticed. One can run for miles each day and still be totally out of touch with the messages the body is giving. The war of mind over body rages in the poshest of fitness centers. The good news, however, is that this destructive process can be reversed. It is possible to establish a loving relationship with one's bodiliness, and through acceptance, awareness and respect to befriend oneself as a spirited body.

Historically, the one generally acceptable source of corporal pleasure could always be found in giving our bodies or using our bodies in the service and care of others. Doubtless, service to others is a precious human gift, but can we really serve, really feel the needs of others when we are ignorant of our own inner wisdom? We can serve out of our own deprivation for only so long. It will surely overtake us in the form of

21

exhaustion, resentment, anger and rage. If, however, we can serve out of generosity to ourselves, out of self-love, drawing from our own corporal wisdom, listening to the language of muscle and blood, then our service to others will not only be fruitful but less tiring.

Developing a "conscious" body, i.e., developing a healthy awareness of one's body and heeding its messages, is the first step to befriending one's body-self. Calming the clamor of the mind with breath and movement restores the human balance and results in an epiphany of the spirit—a true sign of well-being.

The Wisdom of the Body

Recognizing the sacredness of the body and discovering that the body can be a trustworthy friend and wise spiritual guide are the first steps to body wisdom. Full embodied learning takes place when we allow the experience of our bodies to liberate us and transform us into healthy, creative, courageous and peaceful persons.

The Indian poet Kabir writes, "Friend, jump into experience while you are alive!" When we "jump into" the experience of our bodily selves, everyone and everything around us benefits.

> *God, guard me from those thoughts*
>
> *men think in the mind alone.*
>
> *He that sings a lasting song,*
>
> *thinks in a marrow bone.*
>
> —*W. B. Yeats*

Among many today there is a yeasty yearning to find the sacred within the terrible beauty and sensuousness of the body, within the "marrow bone." The awesome presence of the Divine cannot be adequately tasted and known with just the eye and ear. We must knead the cellular, sinewy flesh of the human body to discover the presence and hear the sound of God breathing in our own skin.

Notes

1. Frances M. Tappan, *Healing Massage Techniques: Holistic, Classic and Emerging Methods* (Norwalk, Conn.: Appleton & Lange, 1988), pp. 5-9.

2. Julie Fretzin, "The Body as Healer of the Spirit: An Interview with Mary Ann Finch," *Creation Spirituality* 8, no.1 (January-February 1992): 37.

3. James Nelson, *Between Two Gardens.: Reflections on Sexuality and Religious Experience* (New York: Pilgrim Press,1983), p. 18.

4. Tedi Dunn, "Massage Humanizes Hospital Care: The Planetree Model," *AHP Perspective.* March-April 1989.

5. Ashley Montagu, *Touching: The Human Significance of Skin* (New York: Harper & Row, 1972).

6. Dawn Nelson, *Compassionate Touch.: Hands on Caregiving for the Elderly, the Ill and the Dying* (Barrytown, NY: Stations Hill Press, 1994), pp.19 and 33.

7. John Fenton, *Theology of the Body* (Philadelphia: Westminster Press,1974), p. 130.

8. Mary Ann Finch, "Befriending the Body," *The Way: A Review of Contemporary Spirituality* 29. no.1 (January 1985), p. 60.

9. John Mabry, "There Is No Salvation apart from the Body," *Creation Spirituality*, May 1991, p. 37.

10. Norman O. Brown, *Love's Body* (New York: Vintage books, 1996), p. 221.

Back

*H*ow awesome is the back! How sensuous its curves, how complex its structure, how mysterious its energies! And yet for all its beauty and aliveness, it is "back" there behind us, mostly unseen and untouched except by another. The back is a faithful servant, and sometimes a "suffering servant" that supports the weight of the body's "scaffolding" — its muscles and bones.

The backbone (vertical column) has been characterized as a sacred "pillar of fire." An important part of the back's work is to hold...and hold...and hold. One out of every two adults will suffer some kind of back pain or ailment, often from the tension of holding. A few moments of caring touch can provide a respite, relaxing the tension that results from holding too much for too long. Our backs hold not only our own physical and spiritual weight, but give us the capacity to hold the weight of others as well; to support others in moments of physical exhaustion, mental and emotional upheaval or spiritual darkness. Massaging another's back can be a compassionate and tender way of offering to "hold" another's life for a little while.

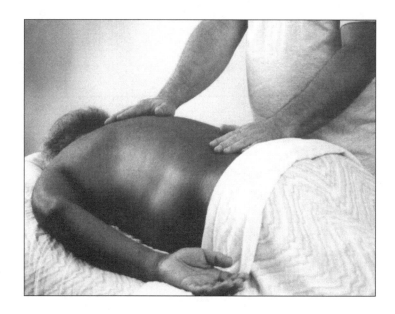

Benefits of Back Massage

◆ Helps prevent back injuries and other problems by relaxing tightly held muscles and by helping the back maintain a sense of flexibility and alignment.

◆ Plays an important role in healing and relieving chronic back conditions by prompting the increased flow of blood, oxygen and lymph that are the body's healing medicines.

◆ Helps counteract the downward pull of gravity on the body; gravity's pull causes the muscles and connective tissue to compress around the spine, creating stiffness in muscles and joints and shortening of the spine.

◆ Helps smooth out muscle spasms, a condition that occurs when muscle fibers become contracted.

◆ Relieves muscle tension and pain associated with structural problems of the back such as scoliosis and dowager's hump.

◆ Relieves low back pain associated with structural malformations such as herniated and degenerative disc diseases.

◆ Eases ordinary muscular tiredness and soreness and is especially helpful for relieving the fatigue from over-working and over-worrying.

◆ Quiets the body and mind and prepares one for rest or activity.

◆ Brings into the body and mind feelings of peace and well-being that are vital to preventing illness and affecting healing.

Conditions, Precautions and Modifications for Back Massage

◆ Never apply direct pressure to the spine. Be especially careful if there is pain in the spinal column, as opposed to the muscle and soft tissue. Spinal pain usually indicates a structural problem, a degenerative disease or an organic problem.

◆ In working with people who have any kind of spinal condition, positioning is very important when massaging on a table. Lying on the side is best. If a person is resting on the abdomen, then the placement of pillows for additional support is very important.

a) side position: support the natural curvature of the spine by placing a pillow between the knees for comfort, another under the head, and a third between the arm and chest (the hug pillow).

b) lying on the stomach: place a pillow under the ankles and a small pillow or folded towel under the abdomen to help support the spine.

◆ Never massage a low back injury while it is inflamed or swollen. Wait at least 48 hours after an injury such as a strain or sprain. Gentle touch, however, such as holding, resting or laying on of hands can be very beneficial and healing.

◆ Be careful not to exert a lot of pressure with people who have osteoporosis, as the bones may be very fragile.

◆ Do not apply forceful pressure over the kidneys.

◆ Never massage over or around the area of a tumor or a raised area of any kind.

◆ If a person is bedridden take care to observe the condition of the skin particularly in the low back. Skin discolorations may indicate a lack of circulation due to the constant pressure of lying in one position. Gentle massage around the reddened area providing the skin is not broken and there is no swelling can be very soothing and can help improve circulation. However, never massage over rashes, broken skin, or bedsores.

◆ Psoriasis is a chronic and recurrent skin condition that resembles a rash characterized by dry scaling. It is not contagious; therefore it can be touched without fear of infecting it or spreading it.

The design of the human back is truly an awesome and wondrous work of the Creator's hand.

Bones

Vertebral Column

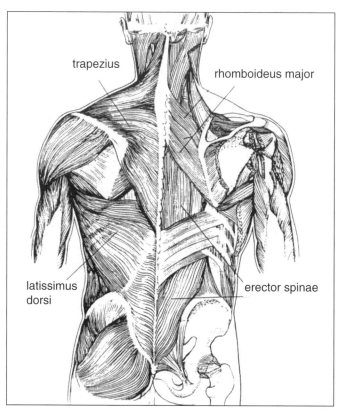

The back bone is the most predominant of all the body's bones. It consists of a column of bones, called vertebrae. Twenty four vertebrae are arranged in three curves:

◆ 7 cervical vertebrae: from base of head to top of back

◆ 12 thoracic vertebrae: from top of back to mid-back

◆ 5 lumbar vertebrae: from mid-back to low-back

The remainder of the column consists of:

◆ sacrum: a flat triangular bone consisting of 5 fused vertebrae

◆ coccyx: a tail bone made up of 4 fused vertebrae

Discs are spongy connective tissue that act as shock absorbers between the vertebrae. They absorb excessive amounts of pressure while walking, jumping, climbing, as well as the pressure of gravity when we're standing still.

The **spinal cord** is a thick strand of nerve tissues that threads itself through holes in the vertebrae. These nerve tissues send information, in the form of nerve impulses to and from the body's muscles, and convey information from our senses to the brain.

Scapula (shoulder blade): is a triangular wing-shaped bone on either side of the spine.

Thorax (rib cage):is a cage-like structure that protects the heart and lungs. It consists of 12 bones on either side of the body that attach to the spine in the back, and the sternum (breastbone) in the front.

The **pelvis** (iliac crest) is a bowl-like structure that holds the digestive and reproductive organs. The back half of the pelvis connects to the back on either side of the sacrum.

Muscles

More than 80 muscles spread out over the back. The following are the main muscles you will be touching and manipulating while giving a back massage. Through relaxation a good back massage will benefit all the surrounding muscles.

The **trapezius** (neck/shoulder muscles) run down either side of the neck, spread out over the tops of the shoulders and stretch mid-way down the back. They help the neck extend and bend from side to side.

Latissimus dorsi (side muscles of the back) are beautiful sheaths of muscles that run all the way up from the low back to under the armpit. They are often referred to as the "pulling" muscles.

Erector spinae (spinal muscles) are rope-like muscles that border either side of the spine. Their primary task is to help us stand tall.

Preparations for Massaging the Back from a Chair Position

Position

If possible have the person sit sideways on a straight-back chair, or in a low-back chair facing a table or desk. Place a pillow for the head on the table so the person's head can rest when needed throughout the sequence.

Another option is to have the person straddle a straight-back chair, providing this is comfortable. Pad the back of the chair with a bed-size pillow so that part of the pillow can fold over the top of the chair cushioning the chest, head and arms when leaning forward.

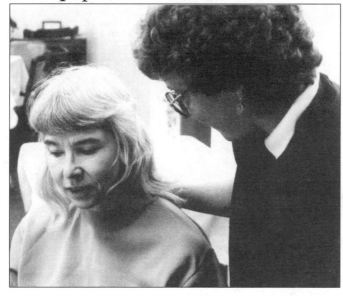

Equipment and Environment

◆ pillows

◆ towels

◆ tape recorder and soothing music, if desired

If it's appropriate provide a symbol reflecting the goodness and beauty of life: a vase of flowers, a candle, a picture that might embody the spirit of caring through touch.

Assessment

Spend a few minutes gathering information about the person's back, and general health so that you can work with a greater sense of compassion. Focus on how the massage can bring the most benefit by asking questions such as "Is there anything you would like to tell me about your back today? Are there any areas that are particularly sore? Have you had any recent injuries or surgeries on your back?" Your interest and willingness to listen is another way of touching.

The Massage Sequence
Lord, make me a channel of your peace. – St. Francis

Centering

1 Once the receiver has settled into a position that is comfortable, step back and take a minute to settle into yourself. Notice if anything is keeping you from giving your full attention to this person and make a conscious decision to set these concerns aside for the time being. Become aware of your breathing; relax! Recall the needs and concerns this person shared with you. Ask the Divine Presence to guide you, and to touch this person through you. "Make me a channel of your peace." Then

let your hands, like warm sunlight, quietly and gently come to rest on the shoulders. Remain here for a few seconds, letting this connection take root. Notice the rise and fall of the shoulders on the breath.

Positioning

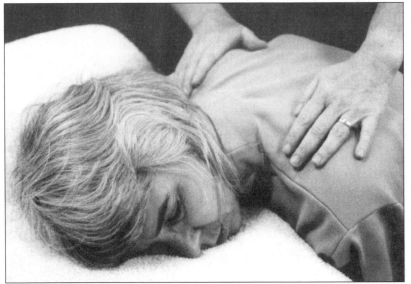

2 Ask the receiver to lean forward and rest the head on the table (and pillow). Return your hands to the shoulders.

Brushing

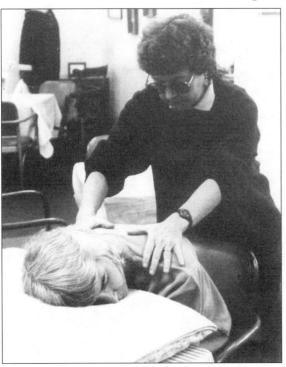

3 Begin by slowly brushing your hands out over and around the shoulders,

4 and down the back as far as you can comfortably reach.

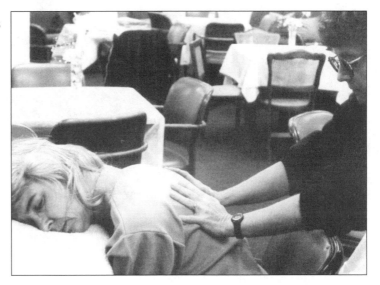

5 then slide your hands up the sides of the body to under the arms,

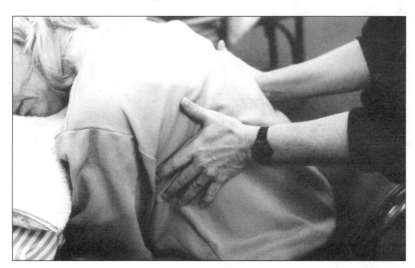

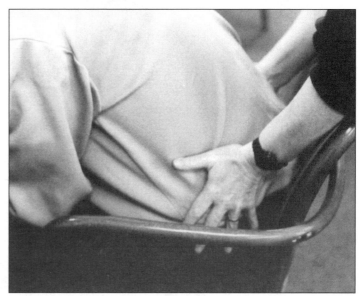

6 and brush firmly down the sides to the tops of the hips. Repeat this brushing stroke several times.

Palm Circling

7 Place the palms of your hands side by side at the top of the back on either side of the spine. Do slow palm circles down the back

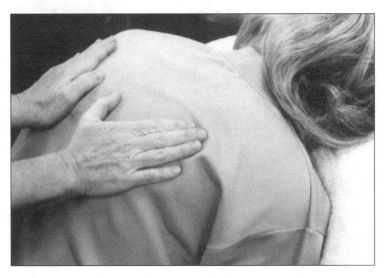

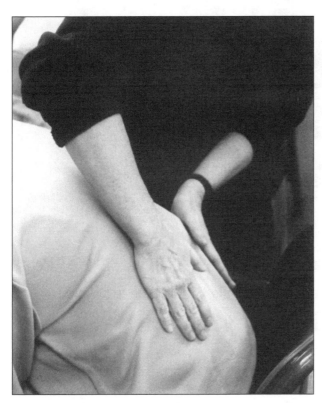

8 To work more effectively in the lower part of the back and over the hips, it is best to adjust your posture by stepping to the side of the chair and facing the back.

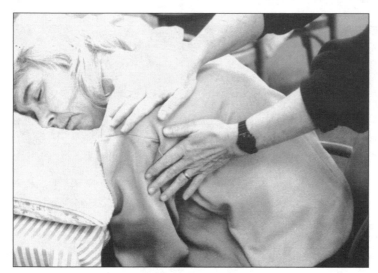

9 Continue the palm-circling action up the far side of the body to the shoulders, across the shoulders,

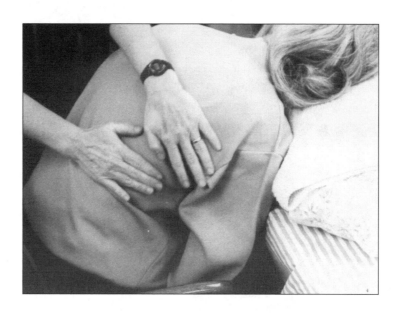

10 and down the opposite side. Adjust your own posture in whatever ways you need to as you continue the palm-circling strokes around the circumference of the back. Involve every part of your body in this circular motion. This generous way of stroking can be both energizing as well as soothing and deeply comforting.

Thumb Circling along the Spine (Erector Spinae Muscles)

1 Rest your thumbs on the rope-like muscles that run along both sides of the spine (erector spinae muscles). Slowly lean forward and with the weight of your body (not just your fingers), press into the muscles under your thumbs and make slow circular movements about the size

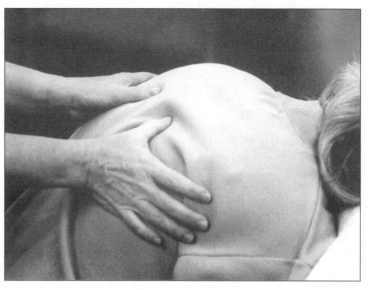

of a quarter. Work slowly and thoroughly from the upper back to the waist. These muscles are like sentinels that guard the sacred pillar of the body. If you work with sensitivity and care here, you may feel the guardedness soften to your touch and notice little releases in the muscle fibers beneath your thumbs. Be aware of your breathing while you're working so your body stays relaxed and your heart remains open and fresh; encourage the receiver to do the same thing.

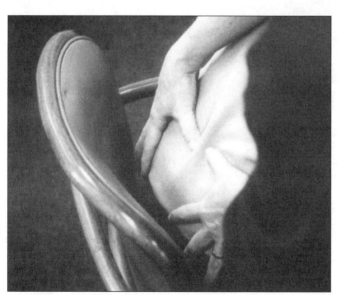

12 As you approach the lower back adjust your posture by stepping to the side of the chair and reaching down into the lower back as is demonstrated in the photo. This position will enable you to apply the appropriate pressure without straining your own body. If your hands and particularly your thumbs tire while doing this work,

pause for a moment, and shake them a little before continuing on. (You can vary this stroke by moving both thumbs simultaneously, or in an alternating fashion, first one thumb and then the other.)

Lean/Hold/Release

13 Use the thumbs and backs of the second and third fingers to work along the erector spinae muscles from upper back to waist. Establish a pattern here of "leaning-holding-releasing." Coordinate this pattern with your breathing: exhale as you lean and hold; inhale as you slowly release.

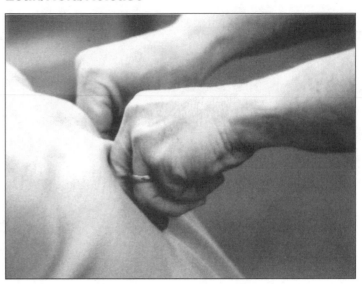

Brushing/Flowing

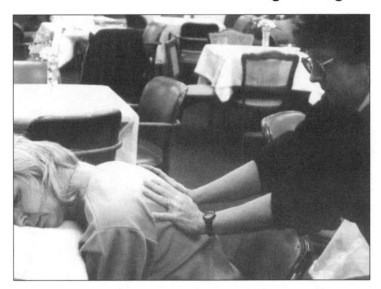

14 Rest your hands on the shoulders. Lean into the palms of your hands and brush down the back. Imagine the receiver's tiredness and concerns flowing away, sinking into the earth. Repeat this three to four times. Let go of all effort whatsoever, and let the movement flow freely.

Rest!

15 Ask the receiver to sit up slowly; rest your hands on the shoulders. Feel your interdependence. Together you are sharing the same life, the same breath and the same spirit.

Circling the Scapula

16 Step to the side of the chair and slide your hand across the upper part of the chest to the shoulder opposite you (your arm will be resting just below the collar bones). Now place your other hand on the back of the opposite shoulder and do slow palm circling all across the shoulder blade (scapula) and between the scapula and the spine (erector spinae muscles). Let your supporting arm remain strong, but not hard or rigid.

Holding the Center

17 Draw your hands to the centers of the upper chest and back. Hold the heart center for thirty to sixty seconds. Pour out the totality of your love.

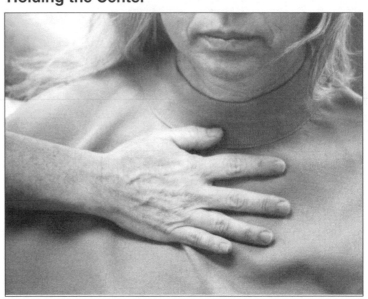

Opening the Wing

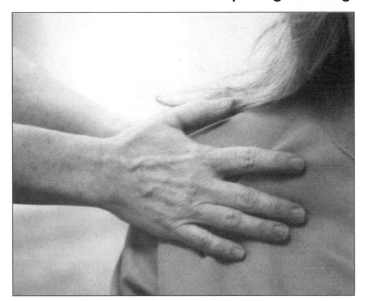

18 Slowly draw both hands out to the edge of the shoulder and off as if you were spreading open the wing of a bird.

Transitioning

19 Step back behind the receiver, and let your hands rest on the shoulders.

20 Step to the opposite side and repeat steps sixteen through eighteen.

Resting

21 Rest your hands on the shoulders. Rest in God; be assimilated into God. Quietly withdraw your hands.

Bowing

Peace to you!
Peace to all!

Preparations for Giving a Back Massage on the Table Position

A common way to give a back massage is to have a person lie face down (prone position) on a firm and comfortably padded table such as a massage table, or on the floor. When using the floor, cover the area with a thick piece of foam padding to adequately support the body. Cover the pad

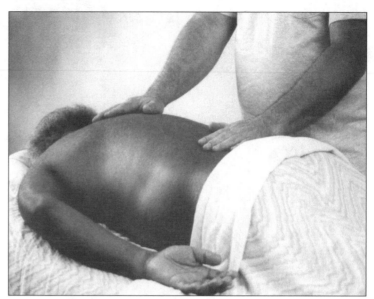

with soft cotton or flannel sheets. If the prone position places undue pressure on the back, have the person turn to the side, giving support with plenty of comfortable pillows, one between the legs, another beneath the head, and a third between the arm and chest (the hug pillow).

Equipment and Environment

◆ table and padding: A padded table that is about 6 feet long and about 30 inches wide is ideal for massage. Otherwise, use a 2-3 inch foam pad on the floor.

◆ pillows and towels: Position a pillow under the ankles to assist with relieving any low back pressure. If a face cradle (which is apart of a professional massage table) is not being used, you may want to put a comfortable bed pillow under the shoulders and chest for additional support. If there is still any discomfort in the lower back, place a soft folded towel under the waist.

◆ oil or lotion

◆ tape recorder and quiet music, if desired

◆ an appropriate symbol reflecting the sacredness and beauty of life: a flower, candle, picture of a sacred place, of a holy being.

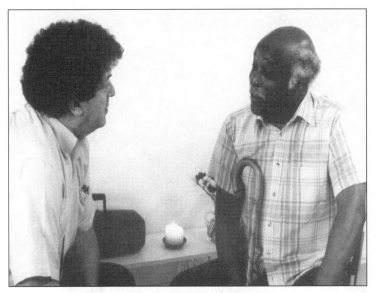

Spend a couple of minutes assessing the needs of your partner. Inquire about any recent injuries or surgeries; ask about any areas of the back that seem particularly tense tired or aching.

The Massage Sequence for the Table Position

There is in all visible things. . . a hidden wholeness.
— Thomas Merton

Centering

As a giver, take a moment to relax your body, to open your shoulders, soften your neck, flex your knees, and allow the weight of your body to drop into the earth. Notice your breathing; let go of distracting thoughts and focus your mind on your intention to care.

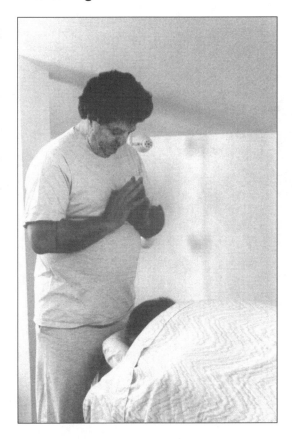

Laying on of Hands (over the sheet)

1 Let your hands rest over the sheet on your partner's back. Listen through your still fingers to the subtle rhythm of this person's breathing. Receive your partner's life into your hands with unconditional love. Let it be a time of quiet prayer for both of you.

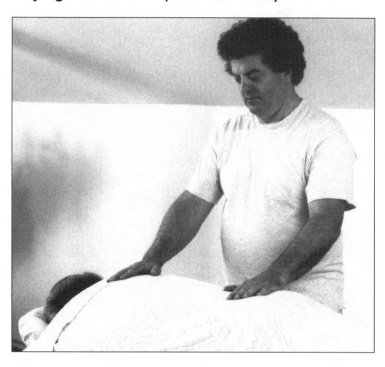

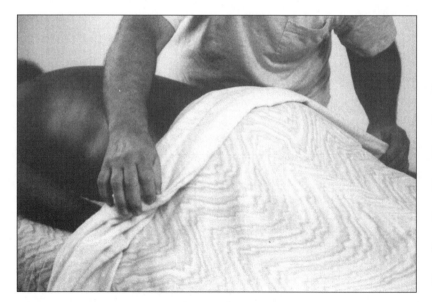

2 Carefully fold the sheet down to the crest of the buttocks. Pour oil into your hands and rub it in thoroughly. Be careful not to do this over the receiver's body, as a single drop of oil on the skin can be quite startling.

Gliding Stroke (Blessing in Motion)

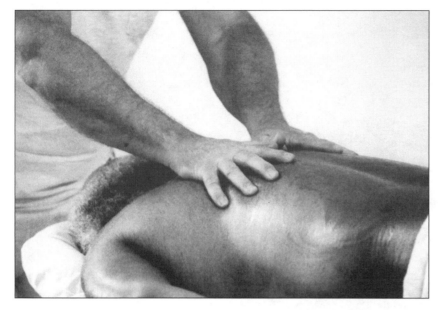

3 Stand at the head of the table. Let your hands settle on the receiver's shoulders. Lean forward and allow the weight of your body to slowly glide your hands down the back to the waist.

4 Slide your hands apart and move out across the low back to the sides of the body;

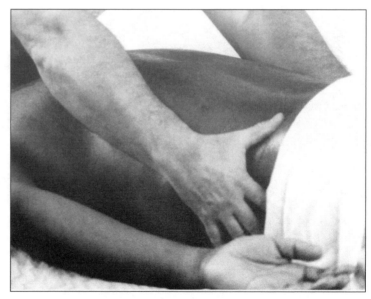

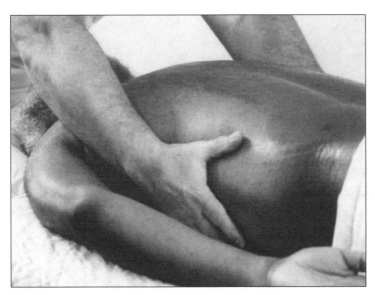

5 Pull your hands slowly and firmly up the sides to just below the scapula (shoulder blades).

6 Slide the hands up onto the upper back,

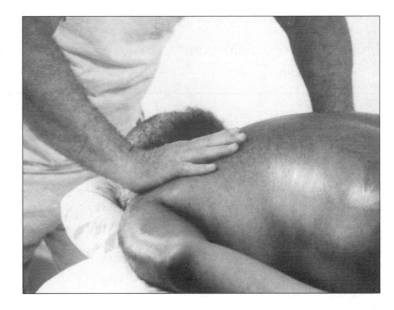

7 and press firmly out over the tops of the shoulders and down over the back of the upper arms.

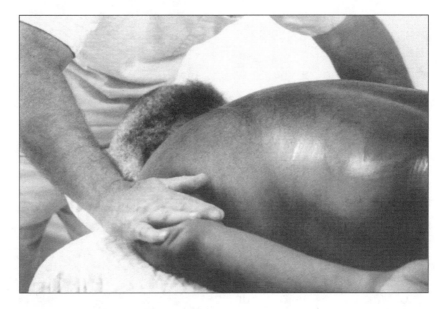

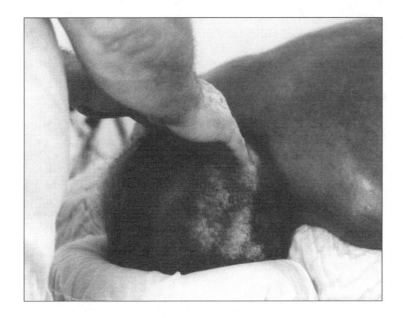

8 Draw your hands back up onto the shoulders and around the back of the neck. Gently squeeze the neck muscles. Repeat this rhythmic and flowing dance-like stroke several times. Let each time be unique as you respond to the information coming to you from the body. Often you will hear a sigh of relief. Trust your heart to guide your hands to do what is best.

Low Back Circling

9 Stand at the side of the table opposite the receiver's waist. Rest the palm of one hand over the back of the other and slowly circle around this flat triangular-shaped bone (the sacrum), that helps to form the back of the pelvis. You can also use your thumbs, and the tips of your fingers to sink into the muscles here.

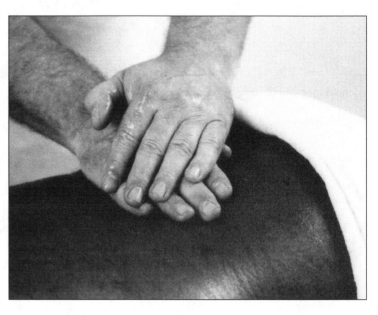

The warmth and pressure of your hands will help increase the circulation process, which in turn will help to relax and stretch the ligaments and muscles around the sacral bone and the pelvis. If the person has chronic low back pain, check concerning the amount of pressure you are using. Be fully present.

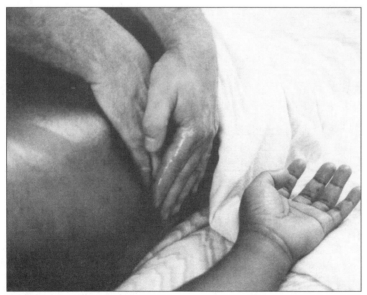

10 Palm circle over both sides of the pelvis. Keep the pressure firm and steady, and remain aware of your own breathing as you work. Attentive breathing will help you sustain your level of energy and focus your attention.

Thumb Circling the Erector Spinae

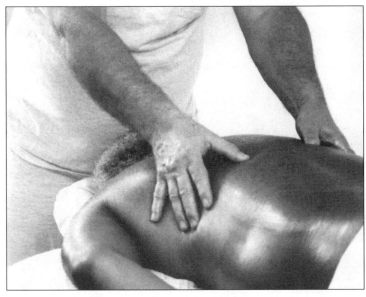

11 Lean the weight of your body into your thumbs as you slowly and rhythmically circle them down along the rope-like muscles that border the spine, (erector spinae muscles), from the base of the neck to the sacrum. While doing this stroke you might imagine the spine as a graceful long fiddle-fern gradually unwinding and lengthening, enabling the person to move toward a more full, energetic and flexible way of being. When you reach the sacrum, sweep your hands back up the sides of the body and repeat the stroke again.

Gliding Stroke

12 Ease the back after this deeper work, by returning to the gliding stroke. (Steps three through eight)

Shoulder and Upper Back Kneading

13 Step to the side of the table and face the receiver's head. Drape your fingers over the tops of both shoulders to stabilize you as you work, and begin gently but firmly to squeeze and knead the tops of the shoulder muscles (trapezius). Work thoroughly from the sides of the neck

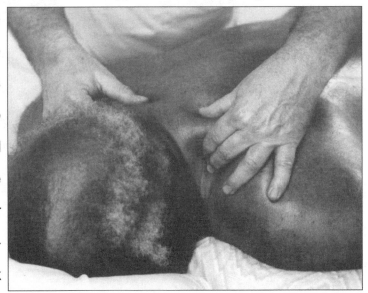

out to the edge of both shoulders. This will help to relieve the tension and stiffness that frequently gets trapped between the neck and the shoulders.

Circling the Shoulders

14 Stand at the side of the table. Reach both hands across to the opposite shoulder, and lay the palm of one hand over the back of the other. Lean the weight of your body into your hands as you do slow circular stroking over the shoulder

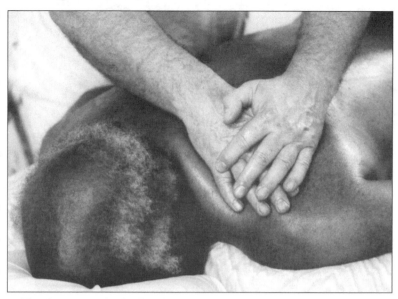

blade and tops of the shoulders. Feel your whole body included in this circular movement. Really move the shoulder muscles; feel the bones, the tendons and ligaments that hold things together. Let one rotation flow into the next as if you were polishing a precious stone.

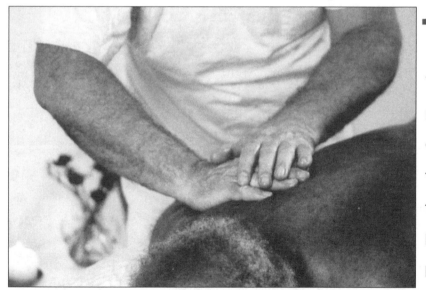

15 Now work on the shoulder nearest you in the same way. This part of the back reflects our heroic efforts to get things "right," and to work things "out." Let your hands compassionately loosen tension and soothe fears. Plant patches of hope in this beautiful and often troublesome part of the body.

Rest!

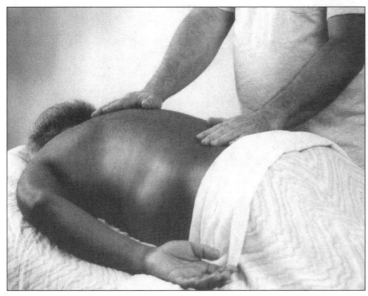

16 When you finish, let your hands rest for a few seconds in the center of the back between the shoulder blades. Visualize peace entering into the blood stream and spreading out into every pore and cell of the body. Imagine it penetrating deep into the mind, anointing it with healthy and hopeful thoughts.

Stroking the Side (Latissimus Dorsi Muscles)

17 Stand at the side of the table beside the receiver's waist. Reach across the table with the hand nearest the receiver's waist. Open your hand and rest it around the waist. Slide your hand upwards from the waist to the armpit.

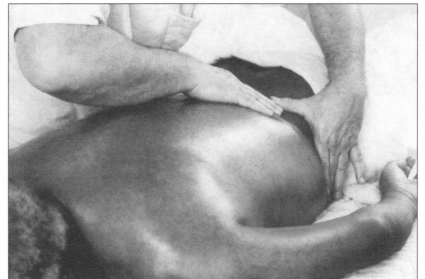

18 Then reverse the stroke by using the other hand to stroke down from the arm pit to the top of the pelvic girdle. Establish a pleasant flowing rhythm as you glide back and forth along these graceful back muscles (latissimus dorsi).

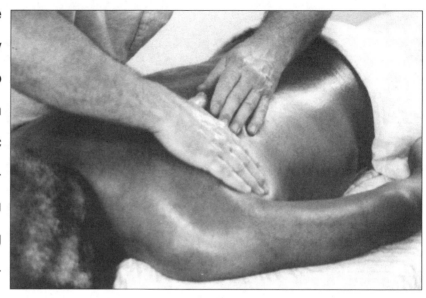

Pulling/Pushing Stroke

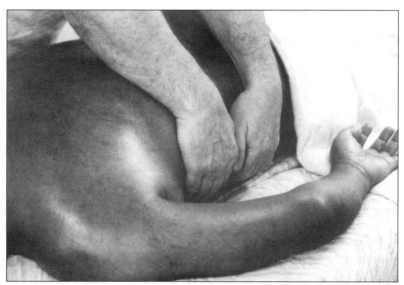

19 Reach across the table and rest the palms of your hands against the side of the back just above the pelvic girdle, fingers pointing down towards the table; bend your knees and sink down into your own legs as you slowly pull your hands across the back and in towards the spine.

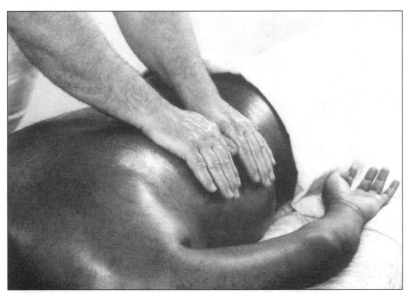

20 Then straighten your legs and lean into the heels of your hands to push away from the spine and over the side of the back. Stroke slowly and rhythmically back and forth, moving up the back from the top of the pelvis to the armpit and down again. Sink into the pulling and lean into the pushing. Bring this movement to a close and step to the opposite side of the table. Repeat steps seventeen through twenty.

Final Blessing and Gliding

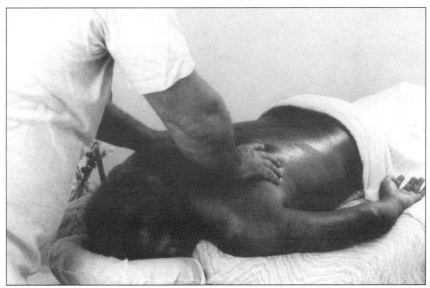

21 Step back to the head of the table and rest your hands on the back of the shoulders. Inhale, and as you exhale, slide your hands down the back to the sacrum; slide your hands out over the top of the pelvic girdle and pull up the sides of the body to the shoulder blades. Draw both hands up to the top of the back; stroke out over the tops of the shoulders and down the backs of the upper arms. Sweep the hands into the sides of the neck, and place them again on the backs of the shoulders. Repeat this blessing stroke two or three times with quiet, loving attention.

Resting!

22 When you finish, reach forward with one hand and rest it softly over the base of the spine. Rest the other hand over the back of the head with the finger tips touching the back of the neck. Imagine a current of healing energy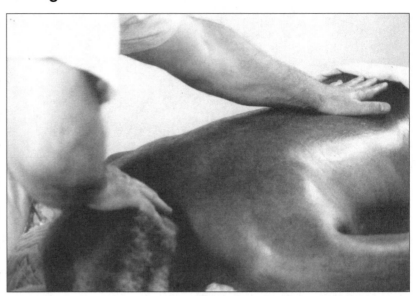
flowing along the spine and radiating out to the whole body. Slowly slide the hand at the base of the spine up the back to meet the hand at the head. Pause for a few seconds and be present.

Draping

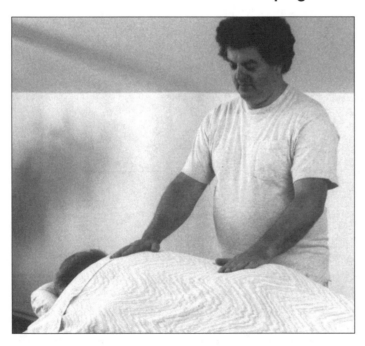

23 Step to the side of the table and carefully cover your partner with the sheet. Slowly withdraw your hands.

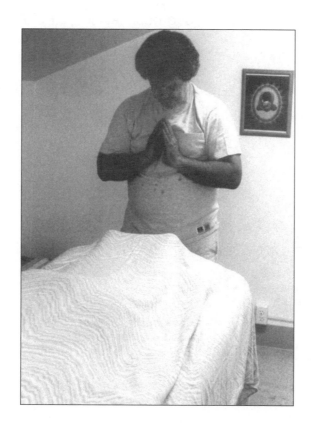

Bowing

Peace to you.
Peace to all!

Legs

Stand for a moment and feel the strength your legs communicate to you . Do you feel stable? Do you feel uncertain? If you walk around for a couple of minutes and notice how your legs propel you through space, do you feel surefooted? Do you feel hesitant? Try moving quickly. Move slowly. Stand still. Compare your ability to stand and to get from place to place with that of someone who gets around with the aid of a wheelchair, a walker or crutches. Imagine what it would be like not to be able to stand at all because you had no legs.

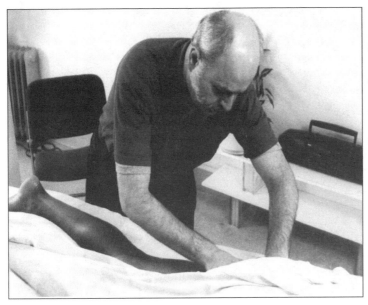

When we gift another person with a leg massage, it is helpful to be aware of the role that legs play in our life and in theirs, and to let our caring be an expression of gratitude for the opportunities we've had to enjoy our freedom. It might also be an opportunity to reflect on how responsibly or irresponsibly we have used that freedom for the sake of others. To "take a stand" for something is an expression frequently used about supporting the basic human rights of those who find it difficult to "stand up for" themselves. Do we take a stand for them? Will we?

Massage can be a spiritual practice for both giver and receiver; it readies and inspires us to "take a stand" both metaphorically and literally, for the well being, and the liberation of all beings, until all beings are free.

Benefits of Leg Massage

◆ Stimulates the flow of body fluids in the legs, which can help alleviate pain and feelings of sluggishness and provide relief from edema and leg ulcers.

◆ Relaxes the hips flexors which in turn will ease tightness and tension in the buttocks and low back.

◆ Relieves pressure on the sciatic nerve, thereby easing sciatic pain.

◆ Eases tension in the muscles surrounding the knee and the knee joint, relieving knee pain and stiffness.

◆ Increases mobility in the ankles; decreases tension in ankles, feet and calves.

◆ Helps relieve muscle spasms and cramps in the calves and hamstrings.

◆ May speed up the healing process of strained or sprained muscles once the inflammation and acute pain has subsided. (See precautions.)

◆ Speeds recovery from muscle fatigue by increasing the supply of oxygen to the tissues.

◆ Relaxes legs over-worked due to:

  • long hours of standing without rest

  • strenuous or repetitive exercise

  • overweight

  • poor postural alignment

◆ Helps relieve emotional tension connected with some of the darker feelings of fear, anger and rage.

◆ Provides a subtle sense of security, power and independence; of grounding and peace.

Conditions, Precautions and Modifications for Leg Massage

◆ Never massage over areas of severe pain. Such pain can indicate a sprain, fracture or break. (Massage can, however, help alleviate severe pain when it is done with skill and care.)

◆ Always support the legs and feet with a pillow in all positions (lying on the back, stomach or in the side position).

◆ Never apply pressure around the joint area if the person has had any injuries or surgeries to the hip, knee or ankle joints.

◆ Be sensitive to the person's sense of privacy in terms of draping. A thoughtful way of preparing the leg for massage is to uncover the lower leg first, followed by the upper leg. Take time to secure the drape well.

◆ Avoid bruises, rashes or any cuts or openings in the skin.

◆ Do not massage recently pulled muscles or tendons.

◆ **Edema**: (abnormal accumulation of fluid in the tissues). Use very slow firm strokes in places where there appears to be a build up of fluids – knees and ankles. When massaging always stoke upwards in the direction of the heart.

◆ **Inflammation**: (redness, swelling, heat and pain in a tissue due to infection or physical injury). Do not apply direct massage to areas of inflammation.

You can, however, move your hands slowly and intentionally over and around the area to move the energy.

◆ **Osteoporosis**: Work gently so as not to fracture brittle bones. Gentle massage to these areas can create sensations of warmth which can feel very comforting and relieve pain. Avoid direct pressure over the spine or any areas of known fractures.

◆ **Sciatica**: Massage the gluteal muscles around the sciatic nerve to relieve pressure on the nerve. Do not apply direct pressure to the nerve itself.

◆ **Sprains**: Do not massage areas of inflammation, that is, where redness and heat are present. However, you can use very light pressure while there is still tenderness and swelling. As the swelling decreases, you can increase the pressure. A sprained muscle cannot recover as long as the fluids are concentrated in one area. Always stroke upwards in the direction of the heart.

◆ **Torn cartilage**: Massage lightly and slowly over these areas.

◆ **Varicose Veins**: Never do deep direct pressure over engorged veins or on a person with a history of varicose veins.

◆ **Thrombophlebitis**: This refers to inflammation of a part of a vein that runs close to the surface of the skin along with the formation of clots in the affected area. Never do direct work in the affected part of the leg because of the possibility of dislodging the clot. When this happens it can travel through the circulatory system to the heart and cause a stroke or death.

◆ **Deep Vein Thrombosis**:This refers to the clotting of blood within the deeper veins of the legs. Never do direct work in the area that is affected.

◆ **Extended periods of bed rest**: Never apply deep pressure to the legs of a person who has been confined to a bed for an extended period of time. The flow of blood tends to become very sluggish when a person is immobile and deep pressure may cause a blood clot to dislodge in the leg.

The Physical Anatomy of the Back of the Legs

The legs are very similar to the arms in anatomical structure except for the fact that the bones and muscles are much longer, broader and heavier. The leg consists of three parts: upper leg, lower leg and foot. For the purposes of massage, I am also including the buttocks in this section.

Buttocks

Bone: The back portion of the pelvic girdle is called the illium. The illium along with the sacrum form the bony structure of the buttocks.

Muscles: The buttock muscles are known as the "gluts." The gluteus maximus/ gluteus medius are broad, thick and fleshy and are the heaviest muscles in the body. Their primary function is to support a variety of leg movements. They fall downward from the crest of the pelvis (ilium) and connect with the upper leg bone (femur).

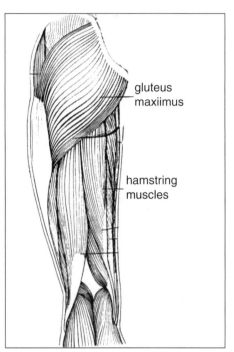

Back of Upper Leg (Thigh):

Bone: The thigh bone is called the femur and is the largest bone in the body. The top (ball) of the femur fits into the side of the pelvic girdle thus creating a ball-in-socket joint. The lower end of the femur connects with the tibia to create the knee joint.

Muscles: The muscles in the back of the leg are massive and strong. The most remarkable group are known as the hamstrings, the longest muscles in the body. They bend the knee and draw the thigh backwards, When these are tight or shortened they can limit the range of motion in the hip joint and put strain on the lower back. Massaging the legs will help relax and lengthen these muscles.

Back of Lower Leg (Calf):

Bones: There are two bones in the lower leg, the larger one is called the tibia (also known as the shin bone). The top of the tibia joins the femur and the bottom connects with the carpal bones to form the ankle joint. The second and smaller bone is the fibula.

Muscles: The two most prominent and superficial muscles here are the gastrocneminus (calf) which extends from behind the knee and attaches itself to the heel bone (calcaneus) by means of the Achilles tendon. The gastrocnemius is a beautiful and powerful muscle that supports and stabilizes the body while extending the foot and raising the heel in walking. Beneath this muscle and lending it support is the soleus which helps to rotate the foot.

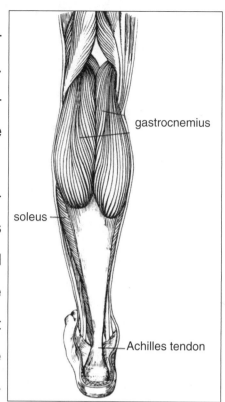

Sole of Foot:

The majority of the foot muscles are located on the bottom of the foot (plantar surface) and are hidden by a thick padding of fibrous tissue. The plantar muscles work to curl and spread the toes and transfer the body's weight from heel to toe with every step.

Nerves/Veins/Arteries:

All of the nerves that transport information from the environment through the muscles to the brain and from the brain back to the muscles in the legs and feet originate in the lower back at the lumbar and sacral areas. Hence the importance of including the buttocks while doing the backs of the legs, providing your partner is comfortable with this.

The major arteries that transport blood through the lower part of the body branch out from the abdominal aorta. However, because of gravity the blood and lymphatic fluids can pool or get backed up here. The pressure of massage strokes, particularly the up and down strokes, is very therapeutic in helping to drain these fluids back in the direction of the abdominal aorta.

Preparations for Massaging the Back of the Leg

Position:

The following sequence describes a process that could be used if a person is able to lie on their stomach either on a table or on a foam mat on the floor. You will want to place a pillow beneath the ankles to assure that the ankles/feet will not be over-extended while lying in this position. If the table has a face cradle this is ideal as it will enable the person to lie face down and breathe comfortably. If there is no face cradle, you will want to instruct the person to turn their head from time to time to keep stiffness from building up in the neck muscles. Sometimes a small pillow or a folded towel under the breasts will also contribute to relieving neck tension. Take the time to make all the adjustments you need both before and throughout the massage; otherwise you will be defeating the purpose of this healing art which is to bring a sense of ease and renewal into the body, mind and spirit.

Equipment and Environment

◆ oil or lotion
◆ candle, fresh flowers, quiet music if appropriate
◆ extra pillows and towels

Assessment

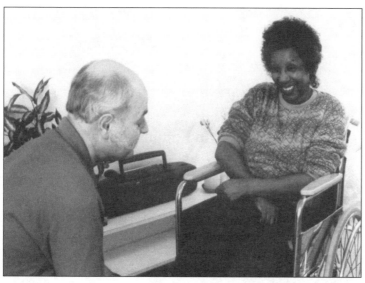

Take a few minutes before beginning the massage to create an environment that engenders trust and love. Gather the information you need about this person's health that will enable you to work effectively and compassionately. Inquire if there is any discomfort or pain in the legs, buttocks or low back, and what, in this person's opinion is its cause. Ask about any past injuries or surgeries. Inquire about his/her health in general. Inquire if the person wants to have the buttock muscles included in the massage. Make it clear they can choose to remove underwear or not.

Create a healing environment through the tone of your voice and softness of your gaze. Maintain a mind that is spacious, nonjudgmental and loving.

Perhaps the most spiritual thing any of us can do
is simply to look through our own eyes.
See with eyes of wholeness
and act with integrity and kindness.
— Jon Kabat-Zinn

The Massage Sequence

This is holy ground...

for the Lord is present

and where God is, is holy.

—Hymn

Centering and Laying on of Hands

1 Stand beside the table. Rest one hand on the buttock and the other on the bottom of the foot. Come fully into your body, and into this moment. Feel relaxed, attentive and prepared to care.

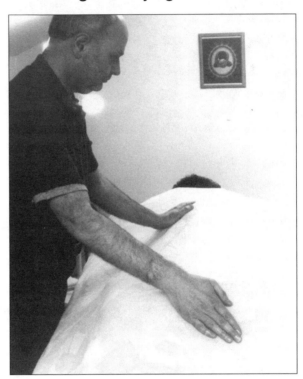

Draping

2 Fold the sheet back first from the foot to behind the knee; then from the back of the knee to the top of the buttock. Let the receiver sense your respect for this sensitive and private part of the body by the careful way in which you secure the sheet both at the top of the hip and between the legs.

Oil and Gliding Stroke

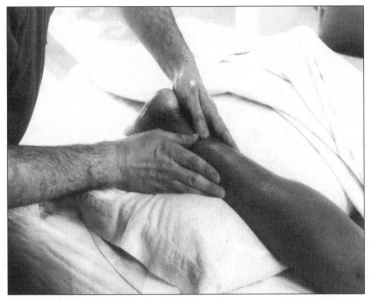

3 Stand near the foot of the table. (Do not stand at the foot of the table as this will prohibit smooth stroking up the leg.) Apply oil and rest your hands on either side of the leg just above the ankle. Position your feet, one ahead of the other, to provide a smooth transfer of body weight throughout the gliding strokes.

4 Move your hands smoothly and slowly up the back of the leg applying firm steady pressure as you pass over the calf muscles and hamstrings. Soften your pressure in the area behind the knee.

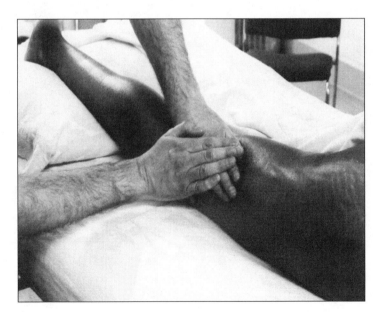

5 Glide directly up over the buttock muscles to the crest of the pelvis. Move the inner hand across the buttock and down to the side of the hip.

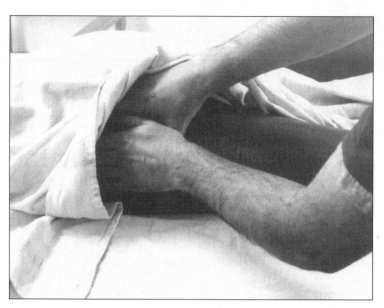

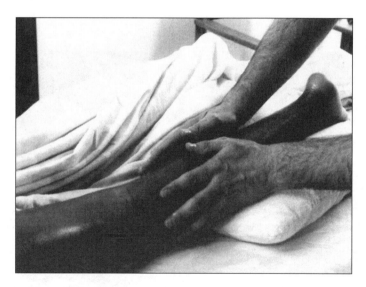

6 In stroking down, let the inner hand cross back over the leg a little ways below the buttocks; draw both hands down the sides of the leg, over the sole of the foot and off. Breathe, and remember: "This is holy ground."

7 Repeat this long, gracious stroke two or three times; remember to let the rest of your body accompany your hands as they apply and release pressure and care deeply.

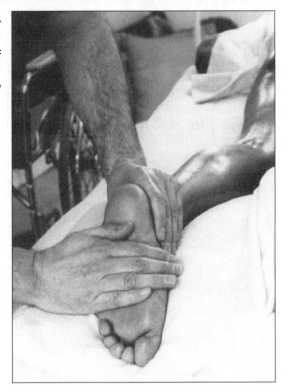

Kneading the Buttocks

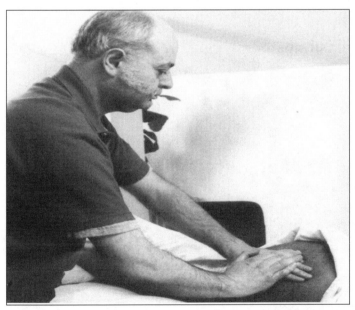

8 Stand beside the table near the buttock (gluteus) muscles. Place your hands one over the other for additional support. Cover the buttock thoroughly with wide, slow and deep palm circles. Always be attentive to what your hands are doing and why. Anoint with respect these muscles that support the trunk of the body.

Kneading the Hamstrings

9 To work more deeply do slow finger and thumb circles around the muscular part of the buttocks. This will help to release tightness in the muscles that surround the sciatic nerve. Be sensitive to any discomfort here; be present, be a blessing.

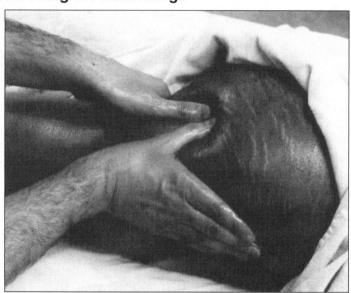

Thumb Circling the Hamstrings

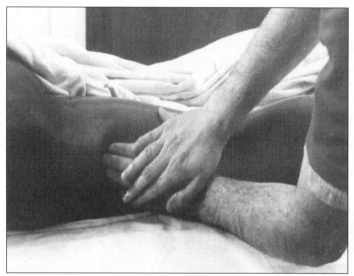

10 Rest one hand over the other on the back of the thigh. Do slow, deep palm circles from behind the knee to the top of the thigh. Be sensitive to the receiver's privacy as you approach the thigh. Circle out and down the outer side of the thigh.

Circling Back of the Knee

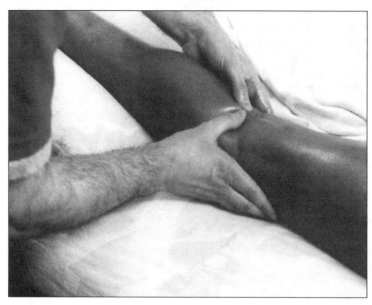

11 Support the sides of the knee with your hands and do small, slow, gentle thumb circles across the back of the knee.

Kneading Back of Lower Leg

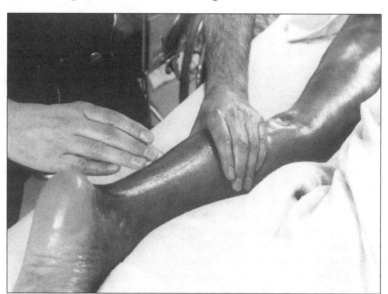

12 Rest both hands on the leg. Grasp the calf muscle in one hand; squeeze it between your thumb and fingers as you slide your hand down towards the ankle; release. Let the other hand repeat the same action sliding back towards the knee. Let your whole body gently sway in rhythm with your hands as they slide back and forth over the leg.

Thumb Circling the Calf

13 Support the sides of the leg with your hands; do slow, deep thumb circles up the center of the calf muscle to below the knee; slide your hands back down the sides of the leg and repeat again. Be sensitive to the amount of pressure your partner can handle here. Remember, your intention is to bring feelings of relaxation and energy into the leg.

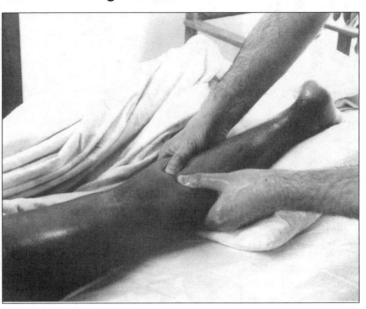

Thumb Circling the Sole of the Foot

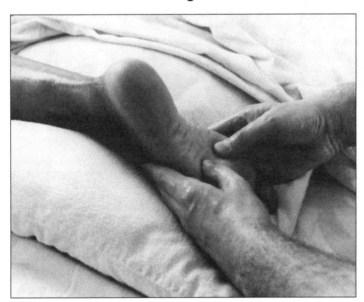

14 Frame the foot between your hands; use your thumbs to make small circling strokes over the muscles in the bottom of the foot, using medium to firm pressure.

Stroking the Sole

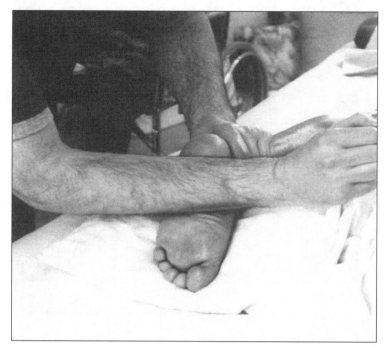

15 Gently stroke back and forth over the sole with the inside of your arm. Be grateful for all the support these feet have been for this person. Be grateful that you can be a source of support now.

Resting

16 Sandwich the foot between your warm, kind hands. Rest for a moment; then slowly let your hands slip off the foot.

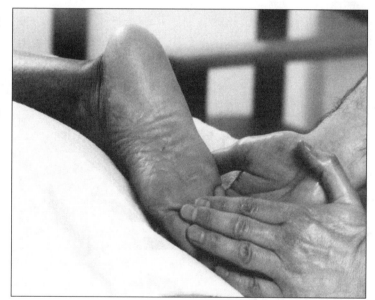

Finishing Stroke

17 Rest your palms on either side of the ankle and stroke upward over the buttock to the crest of the pelvis. Move the inner hand out and down to the side of the hip, and then stroke downward, framing the leg between your hands. Repeat two or three times, lessening your pressure with each stroke.

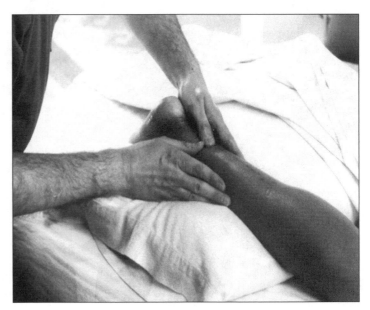

Draping

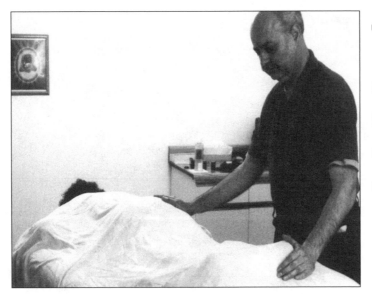

18 Carefully cover the leg and rest one hand on the hip, the other over the sole of the foot for a few seconds; then gently sweep the upper hand down the sheet to the foot and off.

20 Step to the opposite side of the table and repeat the entire sequence.

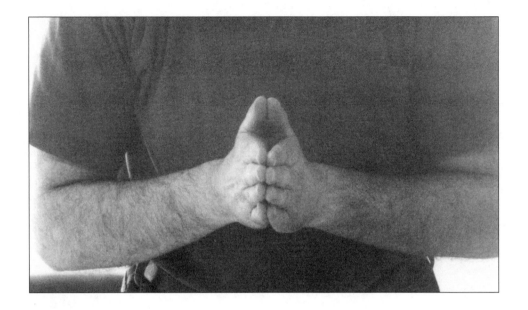

Bowing

This is holy ground...
for the Lord is present
and where God is,
is holy.

The Physical Anatomy of the Front of the Legs

Muscles: The most superficial muscles in the front of the thigh are the quadriceps consisting of four muscles. These are the muscles we utilize when we climb and stride, kick and jump. Because of where they attach in the body, the iliac crest and the tibia, they knit the pelvis and hip to the knee and lower leg.

Knee : The patella is perhaps the most vulnerable joint in the body. The bottom surface of the femur fits into the top end of the tibia to form the knee joint, a hinge joint, which allows the leg to bend/curl backwards.

Front of Upper Leg (Thigh)

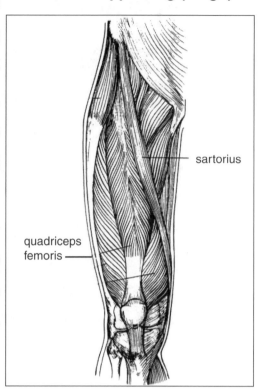

Front of the Lower Leg

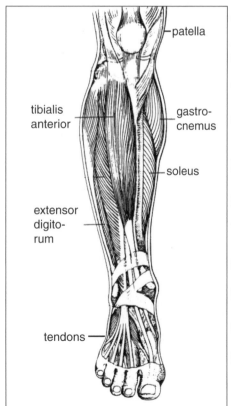

The knee cap (patella) lies in front of the knee joint and protects it from impact. Tendons and ligaments that bind the thigh muscles to the lower leg flow over and around the knee cap.

Muscles: The muscles in the lower leg contribute primarily to the functioning of the foot and ankle. They are responsible for flexing and rotating the foot and raising and lowering the instep (arch). Similar to the forearm, the tendons of these muscles cascade down over the ankle and insert themselves into the toe bones.

Preparations for Massaging the Front of the Leg

Position

To massage the front of the leg the receiver needs to be resting on the back either on a table, a bed, or a foam mat on the floor. Always place a pillow beneath the knees to provide extra support for the low back and to relax the pelvic area. If your partner would like, you can place a folded towel beneath the head which helps relax the neck muscles. For most of the massage, you will need to stand if you are working at a table. However, massaging the feet will provide you with a nice opportunity to kneel down, provided there is sufficient padding for your knees, or to sit on a low stool. Changing positions in this way will help to keep your own body relaxed.

Equipment and Environment

◆ oil/lotion

◆ candle, fresh flowers, quiet music when appropriate

◆ extra pillows, towels

Take a few minutes before beginning the massage to put the person at ease and gather the information that will enable you to work effectively and compassionately. Inquire about any discomfort or pain in the legs and/or feet, and what may be causing it. You can also ask the person about activities that are enjoyable and those that are more difficult. This kind of sharing helps bring attention to the legs

Assessment

in a loving and honest way. Talk to your partner about the ways in which massage might be helpful for the legs as well as for the whole person. Listen to this person with your eyes and heart as well as your ears. The gentle and respectful manner in which you ask your questions and listen to the answers can be very healing for anyone who may be feeling misunderstood, depressed, confused or lonely.

The Massage Sequence

If we have no peace, it is because we have forgotten that we belong to each other.
— Mother Teresa

Centering and Laying on of Hands

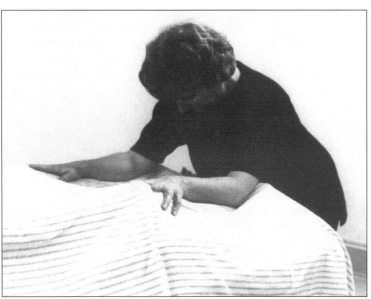

1 Stand at the feet. Lean forward; rest your hands over the knees and your forearms over the shins. Bend low; honor this person. He or she is your brother or sister. Slide your hands over the sheet, down the legs to the tops of the feet. Repeat this blessing in motion two or three times.

2 Stand beside the table and rest your hands on the leg you will be massaging, one hand at the hip and the other over the foot. This quiet way of touching will continue to help focus both you and the receiver.

Uncovering the Leg

3 Draw the sheet back from the leg respectfully, first uncovering the foot to the knee; then from the knee to the thigh. Carefully tuck the sheet between the legs and under the inside of the opposite leg. Treat the sheet as an extension of this person's body. Handle it with the same kind of care and respect that you

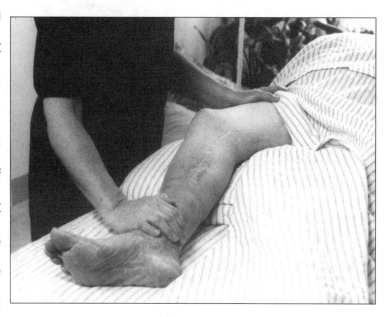

will the leg. Rest your hands on the leg. Breathe. Be in your hands.

Gliding Stroke

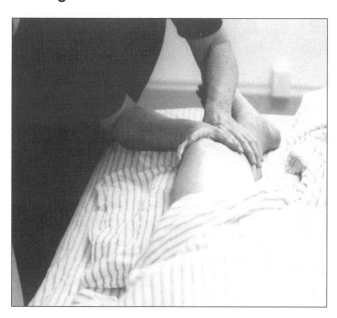

4 Apply oil to your hands. Stand alongside the leg near the foot, (but do not stand at the foot of the table as this will limit the movement of your body during the longer strokes). Rest your hands on the leg just above the ankle; position your feet so that one is ahead of the other. Lean the weight of your body into your hands as you slowly and firmly stroke up the leg in the direction of the heart. Do not apply pressure over the knee.

5 As you approach the upper portion of the leg, draw your inner hand across the top of the thigh to the outer thigh to avoid touching the genitals.

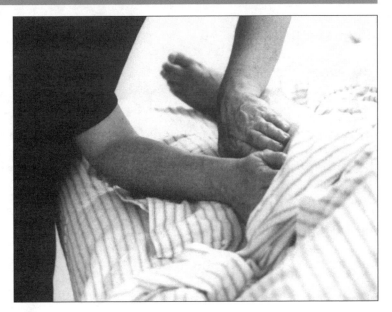

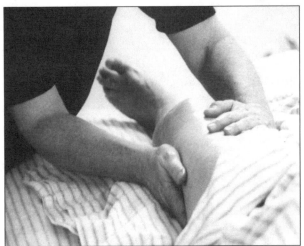

6 To stroke down the leg, move your inner hand back across the top of the thigh. Frame the leg between your arms and hands, and pull down the leg over the foot and off.

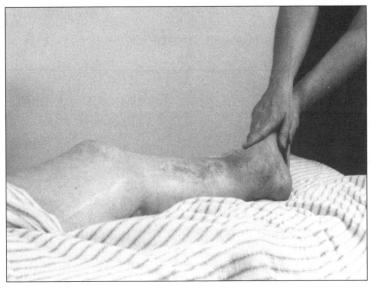

7 Repeat this lovely rhythmic stroke two or three times times, even coordinating the movement with your breathing. It is an excellent way to speed up the blood circulation and bring an immediate sense of warmth and energy into the body. It is also a good way to prepare the leg for the more detailed strokes that are to follow.

Palm Circling the Thigh

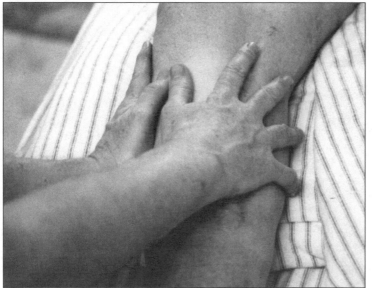

8 Stand alongside the knee. Frame the thigh by resting your hands on either side, thumbs in the center. Beginning just above the knee, lean into the palms of your hands while sliding them from the center to the outer thigh and back to the center again. Move up the thigh in this manner. Slide your hands down the sides of the thigh, stopping just above the knee. Repeat this motion two or three times.

Kneading the Thigh

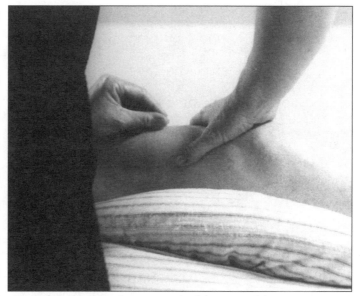

9 Massage the quadriceps (thigh muscles) by lifting up, squeezing and rolling the muscles between your thumbs and fingers, working one hand and then the other. Knead upwards from just above the knee to the upper thigh and back again to the knee. Knead these muscles as thoroughly as you would knead bread dough. Establish a happy and peaceful rhythm to your stroking, and be sure your hips and your shoulders are moving in harmony with your hands. The effect of this total body dance can be both soothing and energizing.

Pulling the Inner Thigh

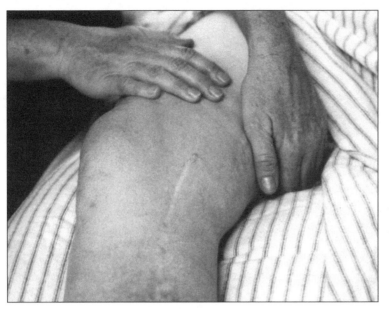

10 Drape your hands carefully across the inner thigh; slowly pull up first with one hand and then the other, working from above the knee to the upper thigh and back to the knee. This movement will help set up a subtle rocking motion in the hip and encourage the release of tension there. Work gently and respectfully as this is a very private and sensitive area of the leg. Honor the receiver's physical condition, the limitations as well as the possibilities.

Circling the Knee

11 Provide the knee with extra support by placing your fingers behind the knee. Place your thumbs below the kneecap; push the thumbs up over the knee and pull them down the sides of the knee. Circle the knee in this manner several times.

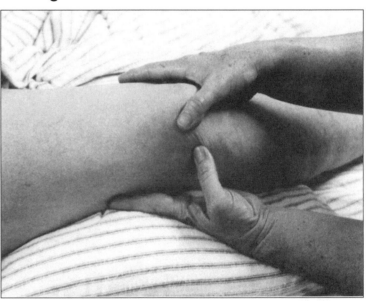

Press gently over the knee cap and more firmly on the muscles above and around the sides of the knee. The knee is a very vulnerable joint that we tend to "lock" when we are feeling frightened or stubborn. Trust the warmth and skill in your hands to unlock whatever tension, fear or holding might be here.

Stroking the Lower Leg

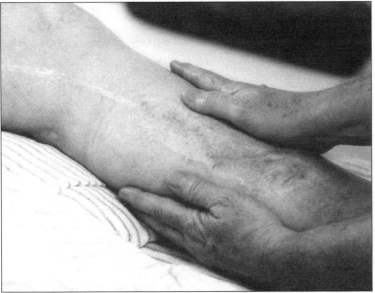

12 Rest the palms of your hands along the sides of the lower leg. Lean the weight of your body into your hands as you stroke upward over the lower leg to the knee. Soften the pressure as you draw the hands back down to the ankles. The slightest amount of pressure here, done with intention and care can bring about feelings of security and affirmation. These feelings can be very healing.

Circling the Ankles

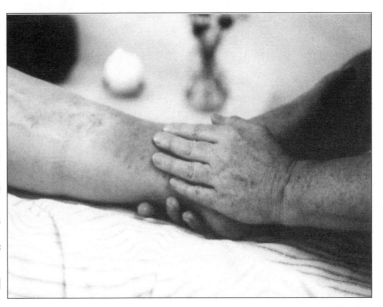

13 Stabilize the ankle by slipping one hand beneath it. Make small slow circles around the bones and ligaments of the ankles. Do one side, then change hands and do the other side of the ankle This will encourage the movement of fluids that tend to pool around the ankles due to lack of exercise or injuries or long term illnesses. Don't be in a hurry; let your movements be slow and soothing.

Stroking the Achilles Tendon

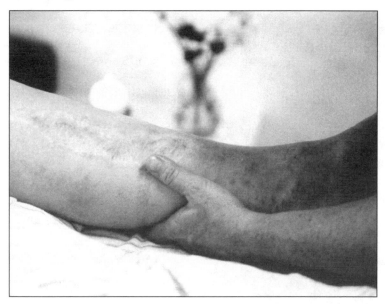

14 Support the foot by wrapping your hand around the heel. With your other hand stroke back and forth along the strongest tendon in the body from just above the heel to mid-calf and back to the heel. Repeat five or six times.

Resting

15 Let the foot nestle between your warm hands. Nothing to do, nothing to fix. This is the ground of the body.

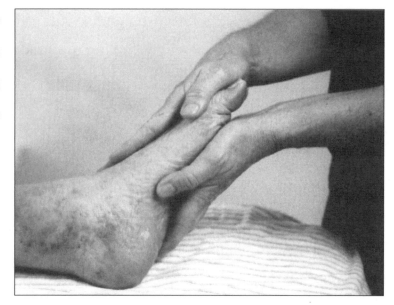

(To continue on with the foot massage, please refer to the Chapter on Feet, page 82.)

Finishing

16 After completing the foot massage, repeat the gliding stroke that you did in the beginning (numbers 4-7) as a way of returning the person's awareness to the whole leg and drawing them into a sense of wholeness and completion.

Draping

17 Draw the sheet back over the leg with the same attentiveness as you have done all of the massage work.

18 Brush your hands softly downward from thigh to the foot several times. Keep wrists and fingers as soft and flowing as your breathing.

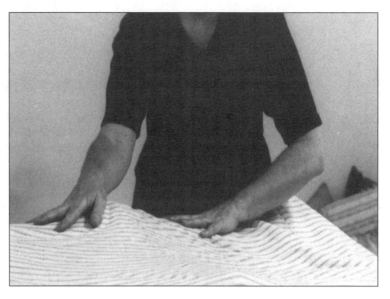

19 Move to the opposite side of the table and repeat the entire sequence.

Bowing

Peace to you
Peace to all!

Feet

*I*f you close your eyes for a moment and let your awareness settle in your feet, you may sense the way they are anchoring you, not only in this physical space but in the global space. Can you feel the immediacy of the earth, the intimacy of this cosmic moment of which you are a part? How does it feel to be standing here, not as an isolated atom, but as an intimate part of the vast world? Does this cause you to be afraid, or does it fill you with curiosity, hope and compassion? Can you stand here with "easy feet," neither grasping the ground nor pushing it away? Our feet have so much to teach us about being in life in both a surefooted and a letting-go way.

Many years ago when my father was dying, he awakened one night with the sensation that his breath was leaving his body. His hands waved frantically in the air before his face, but there was nothing there for him to hold on to. For a moment I caught one of his hands, but he took me with him into his panic. It was only when I 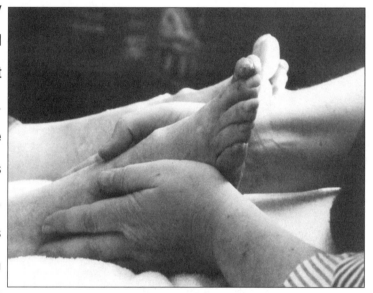 moved to his feet and held them firmly in my hands that he slowly began to relax. As I massaged his feet we celebrated the sacrament of his life and prepared for his death.

There is nothing more relaxing than a caring foot massage. Accumulated tensions and tiredness seem to ooze out of the soles of the feet more than from any other part of the body. The toes uncurl, the arches soften, the ankles relax and the soles open. It can become a deep letting-go practice, a preparation for rest, a preparation for death.

Benefits of Foot Massage

◆ Alleviates tension in the sole of the foot and improves circulation to the small muscles, tendons and ligaments that knit the foot together and support its many actions.

◆ According to a system of massage called foot reflexology which originated in China 5,000 years ago, there are reflex points on the soles of the feet for every major organ, muscle and gland in the body. By stimulating these points through the pressure of massage, the related body parts are toned and balanced. Thus in massaging the feet the entire body benefits generally as well as specifically.

◆ Enhances the functioning of the body's circulatory and lymphatic drainage systems and helps manage a serious health condition known as edema, often seen as a swelling in the ankles and the lower legs due to excessive amounts of fluid.

◆ Eases away the tensions of a hard day's work.

◆ Can be a down-to-earth and wonderful way to communicate love, care and respect for another's life.

◆ Brings a sense of grounding and balance to the whole body.

◆ Is a beautiful and humble act of service; and when done within the context of the art of anointing, it is a way of embodying honor and devotion for the one you are touching.

Conditions, Precautions and Modifications for Foot Massage

◆ **Sensitive feet.** Many people are embarrassed about their feet, and others are very sensitive to touch here. In these cases it is always helpful to start by rubbing the feet slowly and firmly. This will help relax the foot and possibly prepare it for deeper and more intricate probing. If the feet remain sensitive, holding the feet with great care and thoughtfulness can be very calming. Massaging the feet with socks on is another way of caring through touch.

◆ **Dry skin.** The use of a light oil or a natural lotion when giving a foot massage is a compassionate way to treat cracked and dry skin. Be careful not to massage too vigorously wherever the skin is cracked, as this can irritate the condition.

◆ **Athlete's Foot • Toe Funguses.** Usually the person will be quite self-conscious of his or her feet and might be uncomfortable with anyone touching them. Massage, however, can be very helpful for purposes of circulation and healing. If you do massage the feet, massage over socks, or wear gloves to keep the infection from spreading.

◆ **Bunions, calluses, corns, overlapping toes (hammer toes).**

All of these conditions usually respond well to therapeutic touch. It is always important to remind yourself and your partner that you are not here to "fix" or diagnose any condition. Rather, you are involved in a blessing, and one of the greatest of all blessings is that of unconditional acceptance.

◆ **Heel spurs.** A consistent rule of thumb is never to press directly on any area of pain such as the area of the spur. Rather, focus on massaging the muscles that move away from the point of pain, in this case toward the toes.

◆ **Strains and sprains.** Because the foot is so complex and is held together by a large number of tendons and ligaments, sprains and strains are common injuries. Massage should never be done directly on an area that is inflamed due to a strain or sprain. However, gently holding the affected area can generate warmth which will benefit the circulatory process, and help to speed up the elimination of toxic build-up due to the injury. When the swelling and the pain level are reduced, then massage can safely be done, and will contribute greatly to quickening the healing process.

◆ **Swollen ankles**. There are many reasons why the ankles swell, ranging from the pull of gravity upon the body, to being on one's feet for long periods of time, or to being pregnant. These conditions respond well to the pressure that is applied during massage. Gentle flowing movements around the ankle and on up to the knee can be very helpful in stimulating the flow of blood circulation. Other conditions, however, such as injuries, arthritis, and problems that exist in other systems of the body (particularly the cardiovascular system) require more caution. It's important to remember that massage may not affect the swelling if the cause is systemic rather than localized.

◆ **Arthritis.** In general, massage is a soothing and effective way for controlling the pain so frequently associated with arthritis, provided the joints are not inflamed. The warmth that comes from gently holding the inflamed areas can increase circulation and help relieve the pain resulting from the inflammation and the degeneration of the joints and tissues.

The Physical Anatomy of the Feet

Each foot contains 28 bones bound together by 38 muscles and a vast array of ligaments and tendons. An intricate pattern of veins and arteries supplies the foot with blood and oxygen, and carries away the waste products that settle here at the base of the body like sediment at the bottom of a pond.

Nerve endings

The sole of the foot is blanketed by 72,000 nerve endings, making it one of the most sensitive parts of the body. Leonardo da Vinci called the foot "the greatest engineering device in the world."

Bones

The foot bones are arranged in such a way as to support the body's weight while standing and walking, and provide the whole body with the kind of foundation that creates a sense of confidence, stability and maturity.

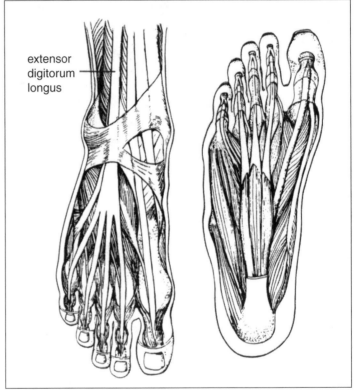

extensor digitorum longus

It's quite amazing to consider that nearly 1/4 of all the body's bones reside here in this relatively small area. With the the exception of the heel bone, the foot bones are arranged in the very same design as the hand.

There are:

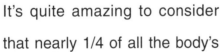

14 toe bones (phalanges)

5 foot bones (metatarsals)

7 ankle bones, including the heel bone (tarsals)

Muscles

Many small muscles control the movements of the foot's bones. The muscles that are responsible for the movement of the toes have tendons that are connected to the foot bones, while the muscles that control the foot bones have tendons that originate in the lower leg. In other words, the classic spiritual had it right:

> The toe bone's connected to the foot bone;
>
> the foot bone to the heel bone,
>
> the heel bone to the ankle bone,
>
> the ankle bone to the leg bone. . .

Achilles Tendon

This is the largest tendon in the body, and it attaches the calf muscle in the lower leg to the heel. Nearly every movement that the foot makes affects this tendon; therefore it is very important to maintain its elasticity.

Preparations for Giving a Foot Massage

Position

A relaxing foot massage can be given to a person while they are resting in bed, sitting in a chair, or lying on a cushioned mat on the floor. It can be given in almost any setting imaginable, at home or at work. Make the effort to find an appropriate place and time, and make sure the position is going to be comfortable for both of you.

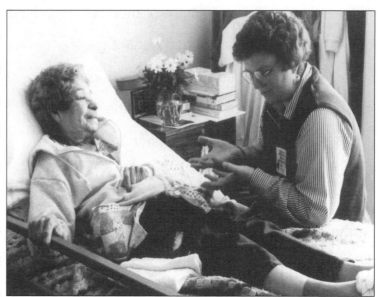

Equipment and Environment

◆ pillows, towels and blankets

It's a good idea always to have a few extra pillows handy for propping up the legs or supporting the head if necessary. Soft large towels provide warmth and further comfort. Place a towel in your lap and under your partner's foot to prevent the oil or lotion from staining your clothes, the carpet or bed linens. Have a throw blanket or large beach towel handy to put around your partner in case they become chilly.

◆ oil or lotion

◆ music and a lighted candle add a sense of the sacred and help to place the massaging in a context of prayer and faith.

Assessment

Before you begin to massage the feet, gather whatever personal information is necessary about your partner's general health, and especially the condition of the feet and legs. This will help you work more intelligently and compassionately. It will also give your partner a sense of confidence and security. If the receiver is concerned about the sensitivity of the feet, discuss the possibilities of massaging over socks. The feet are vital to the body's feeling grounded and stable. It's a real art to be able to quiet and settle nervous feet, to gift the person with a few moments of groundedness. One good experience will help to lessen any fear or hesitation the next time.

Centering

1 Quietly settle your hands over the tops of both feet as a way of establishing a relationship that is one of love, trust and respect. Breathe in a relaxed way and become aware of grounding yourself. Notice your feet; feel them planting you here. Let go of all other thoughts. Be present to the receiver.

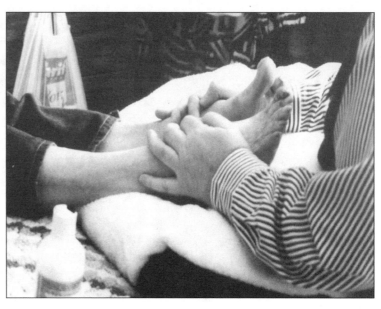

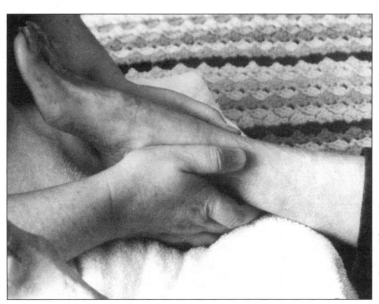

2 Bring both of your hands to one foot; carefully and firmly stroke over the entire area here, from the toes into the ankle and even a little ways up into the lower leg. Squeeze the arches, gently flex and stretch the top of the foot. This is a time for getting acquainted, a time for establishing trust, a time for settling in and preparing the feet for anointing. Don't be afraid to let this person feel your love, and your willingness to minister to him or her in this intimate way. When you've finished with this brief exploration, slowly remove your hands.

Laying on of Hands

3 Apply oil or lotion to your hands, and then approach the receiver's foot and embrace it with your warm hands, one hand supporting the sole and the other hand, resting across the top of the foot. Let your hands remain still for a moment, allowing the person time to settle into your hands and through your hands,

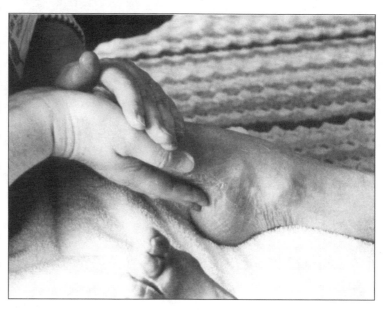

into his or her body. Remember that some people's feet are sensitive and ticklish, so let your hands be relaxed, confident and inviting. Slowly spread the oil by stroking your hands over the entire area of the foot, ankle, and a little way up into the lower leg. Move slowly, gently and rhythmically.

Ankles

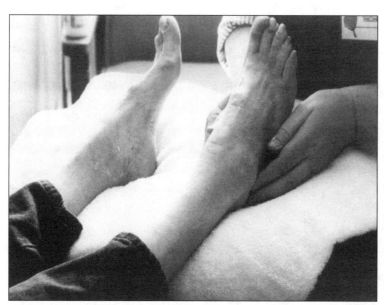

4 Massage the ankles first. Rest both of your hands on either side of the ankles and with your finger tips do slow firm circles all around the ankle bones and the tissue beneath them. Like the wrist, this is an area where many nerves, tendons and muscles in the leg converge on

their way to the foot. It can easily become congested with tension.

5 Cradle the foot between your hands. Do slow thorough thumb circles across the top of the ankle where the foot joins the leg, probe and stroke into the spaces here between the ligaments and tendons. This movement will help to push back into the blood stream the excess fluids and waste products that collect in the ankles due to stiffness and fatigue. This will allow them to be released from the body.

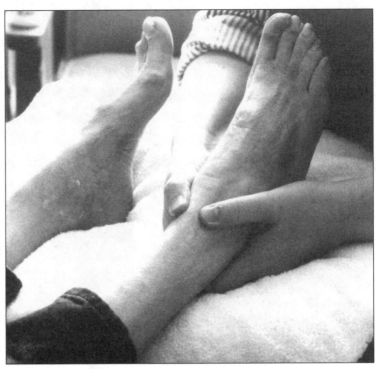

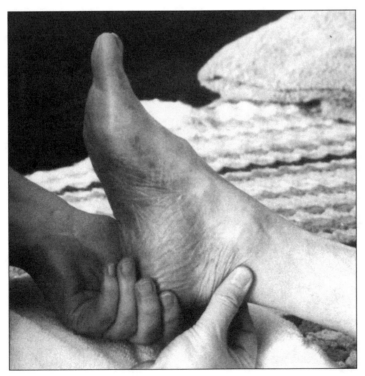

6 Wrap one hand around the back of the heel to provide support; with your other hand stroke the achilles tendon between your thumb and index finger. This area can be quite tender, so be responsive to the receiver's comfort.

Tops of the Feet

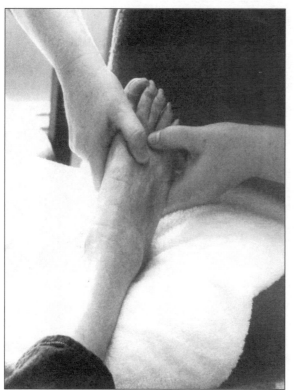

7 Stabilize the foot by wrapping your fingers under the sole. With your thumbs, make small circular movements over the top of the foot, working methodically from the base of the toes back to the ankle. Sink thumb over thumb in the spaces between each foot bone. This part of the foot seldom receives attention other than when we're slipping on socks or tying shoe laces. Work into the little muscles around the base of the toes.

O Lord, you have probed me and you know me. (Psalm 139)

Toes

8 Grasp the sides of each toe gently between your thumb and index finger; carefully stretch and rotate each one, working from the base of the toe. If the person tends to be ticklish, suggest a few deep breaths while you hold the toe. (If the sensitivity persists, move on and massage another part of the foot.)

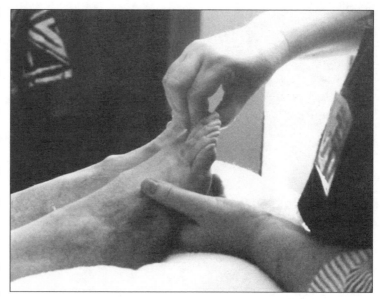

Foot Squeeze

9 Conclude your work on the top of the foot with a good foot squeeze. Grasp the foot with your whole hand just above the ankle, and stroke downward hand over hand from the ankle through the toes. Continue this energetic stroke for a few seconds.

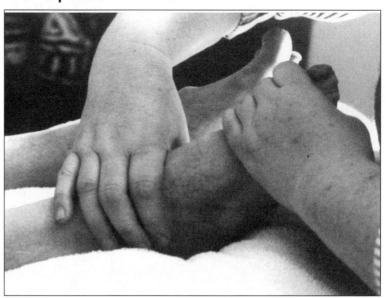

Resting

10 Gracefully massage the entire foot. Notice now naturally your hands mold themselves to the foot's shape as you are stroking it. Now, let your hands come to a rest. Let them be a safe harbor and a reservoir of strength for the foot's tiredness. In this sense anointing the feet, as in all massage, is a true work of mercy.

Sole Work (Thumb Circling)

11 Drape your fingers over the top of the foot to stabilize it. Use your thumbs to do slow thorough thumb circles on the sole of the foot, working from the base of the toes to the heel of the foot.

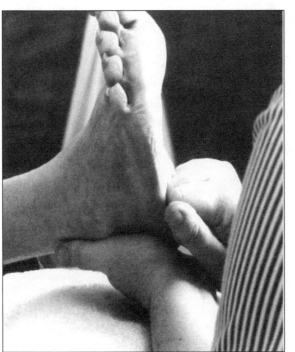

12 Wrap one hand around the back of the foot. Fold your other hand into a soft fist and press the back of your fingers into the heel. Circle the area vigorously. This stroke can be very stimulating and create delicious warm and tingling sensations in the foot.

13 Open your fingers and use the back of your hand to sweep from the heel towards the toes.

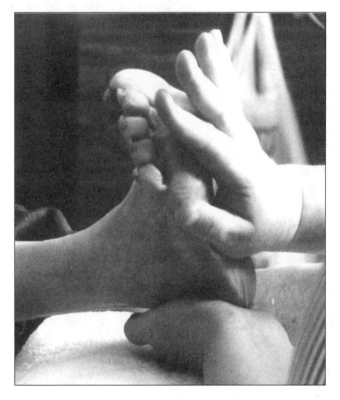

14 Turn your hand over and use the palm of your hand to brush from the toes to the heel. Let your whole upper body move in rhythm with your stroking.

15 Now, spend a couple of minutes caressing the entire foot. Let your hands be free to massage in whatever ways your heart leads them to do. Be sure to include everything: the ankles, the top of the foot, the toes and the sole. Be as generous as you can, with the precious ointment of your love.

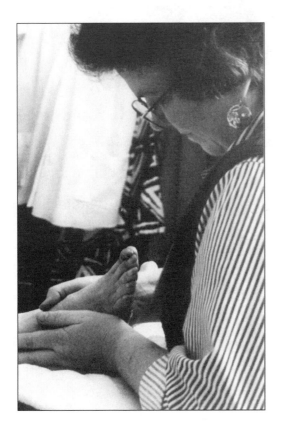

16 Finally, let your hands come quietly to a rest; tenderly hold this foot and the delicate roots of this person's life in your warm and nurturing hands. Relax your shoulders, let your breathing flow easily, and be a channel of peace.

When it feels right, slowly let your hands depart by slipping silently off at the very ends of the toes. With a soft fresh towel, carefully wipe off any excess oil or lotion. Don't hurry; rather let this gesture be a part of the anointing.

17 Repeat the entire sequence on the other foot.

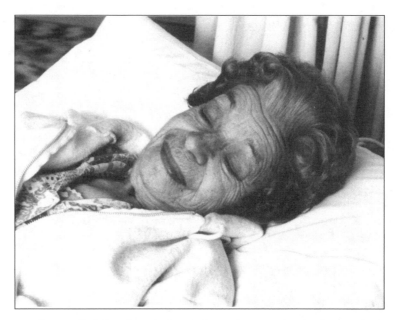

18 When you have finished with both feet, bring the palms of your hands together as you might in prayer, and bow respectfully to your partner. Be grateful for the time you have spent serving and anointing this "body of Christ."

Bowing

Peace to you
Peace to all!

Arms

When you let your arms rest at your sides, do they feel heavy? Sad? Cold? Do they appear to be light? Happy? Warm? When you let your arms rest at your sides, notice the way in which they help to balance your upper body, giving it a sense of alignment, symmetry and gracefulness. Imagine what it might feel like if you had only one of your arms; sense how off-centered or off-balanced that would make you feel. Take a moment to be grateful for your arms. We express our feelings by engaging our arms. They are the visual symbols of our thoughts, wishes and attitudes, both generous and selfish. What actions or non-actions weigh you down? What activities delight and energize you? How do your arms enable you to participate more fully in these actions?

For all the good work they do, our arms seldom receive the attention they deserve. A simple arm massage can be given to someone sitting in a chair, or it can be part of a full body massage. Stroking, squeezing, rocking, wringing the arms are all ways of flushing tiredness out of the muscles. Along with residual toxins, the remnants of selfishness and wrong-doing can also be released. This simple act of caring not only may relieve another's weariness, but might also help prepare them to be more open, generous and responsive to the tiredness of others.

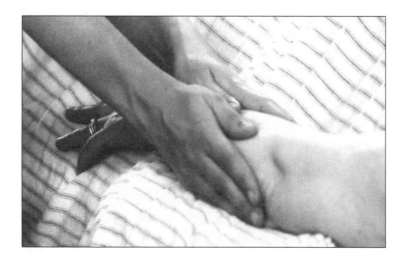

Benefits of Arm Massage

◆ Helps to release tension in the arms and hands caused by detailed and repetitive work such as typing, writing, computer work, sewing, playing musical instruments, or giving a massage.

◆ Helps to release tension and tiredness in the arms due to heavy or concentrated work such as gardening, cleaning or other forms of manual labor.

◆ Releases violent tension in the arms and hands before it has a chance to build up and manifest itself through behavior such as pounding, punching, clutching and striking.

◆ Relieves arthritic stiffness and pain in the shoulders, elbows, wrists and fingers.

◆ Increases the capacity of movement in the shoulders, elbows wrists and fingers, which in turn brings about a satisfying sense of confidence and gracefulness.

◆ Relieves cramps and muscle spasms in the arms and hands by stretching the muscles and increasing oxygenation and circulation to the contracting muscles.

◆ Relieves shoulder and neck tension.

◆ Prepares a person to return to work again with enthusiasm, creativity and peace.

◆ **Restricted Range of Motion:**

Inquire as to whether there is any restricted range of motion due to injury or surgery particularly to the shoulder, elbow, wrist or finger areas.

> For limited range of motion in the shoulder, do very gentle stroking all around the shoulder and upper arm.
>
> For limited range of motion in elbow, do gentle stroking around the elbow and through the crease in the arm.
>
> For limited range of motion in wrist, do gentle rotations and stroking in the forearm near the wrist and palm.

◆ **Bruises and Lesions**: Avoid bruised areas and skin lesions.

◆ **Osteoarthritis in Joints**: If not inflamed, massage thoroughly and gently.

◆ **Inflamed Joints**: Do not apply direct pressure to areas of inflammation; you can, however, move your hands slowly and intentionally over and around the area to move the energy.

◆ **Tendonitis**: Gently rest your hand over the area and let the warmth and comfort from your hands penetrate the area.

◆ **Carpal Tunnel Syndrome**: Work gently throughout the wrist area, forearm and hand; keep checking in with the person so as not to cause discomfort.

The Physical Anatomy of the Arms

The arms are one of the most beautiful and graceful parts of the human body. This is due in part to the weight, size and shape of the bones and muscles, as well as to the various types of joints found here. The arm consists of three parts: upper arm, forearm and hand (the hand is discussed separately in the following chapter).

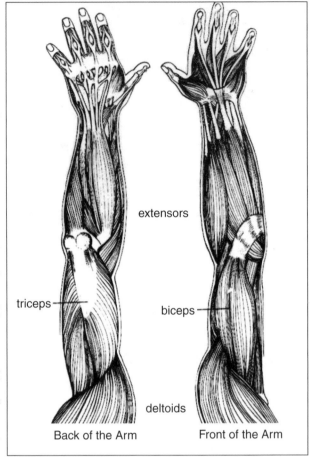

extensors

triceps

biceps

deltoids

Back of the Arm   Front of the Arm

Upper Arm Bone: The largest bone in the arm is called the humerus. The top or "ball" of the humerus fits snugly into the socket of the shoulder blade (scapula). This ball-and-socket joint enables the arm to enjoy a wide range of movements including full rotation depending upon the condition of the joint and its surrounding muscles.

Muscles: The humerus is held in place by several muscles, along with attending tendons and ligaments. The most obvious (superficial) muscles are the deltoids, biceps and triceps. The *deltoid* muscles flow over the top and into the upper portion of the back of the shoulder. They give the shoulder its lovely rounded appearance. Beneath the deltoids on the front of the arm are the *bicep* muscles which bend the arm; a companion to the biceps are the *triceps* on the back of the arm which straighten it.
We utilize these muscles every time we push or pull, lift or lower things.

Forearm

Bones: The bones of the upper and lower arm join together at the elbow to create a *hinge joint.* The hinge joint makes it possible for the arm to bend upward, bringing the hand to the shoulder and back down again. The forearm is made up of two bones: the smaller one which runs along the little finger side is called the *ulna,* and the larger bone, the *radius,* runs along the thumb side of the arm. The ulna and radius meet at the wrist. The radius connects with the wrist bones (carpals), creating a *gliding joint* which enables the hand to twist in many different directions. ("Wrist" is derived from an old English word, *wraestan,* meaning to wrest or twist.)

Muscles: Many of the muscles on the front of the forearm are responsible for flexing the wrist and fingers, while those on the back extend them. Because of this they are often referred to as *extrinsic flexors and extensors.* These muscles are responsible for nearly all the activities our hands are engaged in throughout a single day from the most delicate to the coarsest. All the more reason why everyone from a toddler to an elder would benefit from an arm/hand massage nearly everyday.

Nerves, Veins and Arteries: The *nerves* that inform and activate the arms and hands flow down from either the neck (cervical spine) or from the armpit (brachial plexus).

Several *arteries* carry blood from the heart into the arms and hands. You can feel the pulsing of life through the artery at those places where the artery comes close to the surface of the skin. One of the most well-known arteries in the body is the *radial artery* which runs down the thumb side of the arm. This is the artery we feel when taking a pulse at the wrist. *Veins* in the arms and hands are usually very easy to locate. This bluish network meanders over the hands and pushes the fluids back up the arm into the heart. The long gliding strokes in massage help this process along.

Hands: (See Hand Sequence p. 119.)

Preparations for Giving an Arm and Hand Massage

Position:

Massaging the arms and hands can be done with the receiver lying on the back or the stomach. The more common position is to be resting on the back as is shown in this sequence. Place a pillow under the knees to give additional support to the low back. Decide with the person if they would like a folded towel under the head; sometimes the additional padding and slight lift to the head can help relax the neck muscles.

Your own position may vary throughout the sequence. In doing more detailed work on the hands you may wish to partially sit on the side of the table and support the hand on your knee; if the table is low, you may want to kneel. Placing a folded towel beneath the hand and wrist may protect the wrist from unwanted pressure.

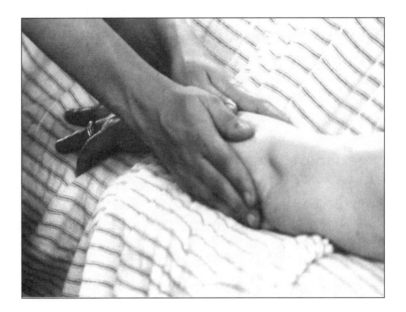

Equipment and Environment:

◆ oil or lotion

◆ candle, fresh flowers, quiet music when appropriate

◆ extra pillows, towels

Assessment

Spend a few minutes before beginning, to gather whatever information is necessary for you to work effectively and compassionately.

A good opening question might be, "Is there anything you would like to tell me about your hands and arms?" Inquire about any injuries and/or chronic conditions such as arthritis or tendonitis. A lovely question that engages the experience of the person in a positive way might be "What kinds of work, and other activities do you like to do with your arms/hands?"

You may want to suggest that this time be an opportunity to let go of the pressures of having to achieve, create or do anything at all; that it be a time of gratefulness, a time of "great fullness."

The Massage Sequence

The Lord is my shepherd,
I need nothing more.
You give me rest...
You revive my drooping spirit."
— Psalm 23

Centering and

Laying on of Hands

1 Stand beside the table. Take a moment to be quiet and to ask yourself, "Am I here? Am I present?" Take the time to consciously come into your hands. Then slowly settle one hand over the shoulder and the other over the back of the hand. Brush down the arm from shoulder to hand. Slip the arm out from beneath the sheet. Apply a little oil to your hands and rest your hands softly upon the arm.

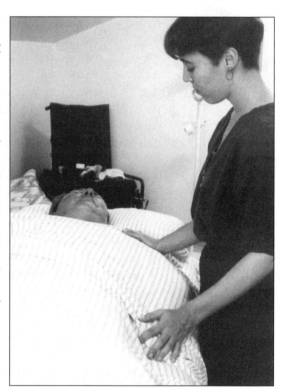

Gliding Stroke

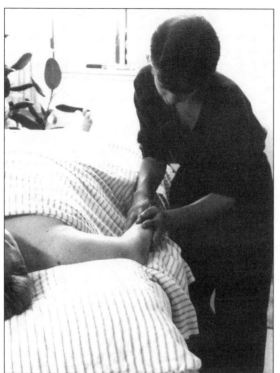

2 Position the palms of your hands just above the wrist, molding them to the shape of the arm. Position your feet so that one is slightly ahead of the other. (This will enable you to use the weight of your body more effectively as you stroke up the length of the arm.) Stroke slowly up the arm; let your whole body come with you, lending more weight and firmness to your hands.

3 Let your hands flow over the shoulder, allowing a ray of warmth to penetrate the joint.

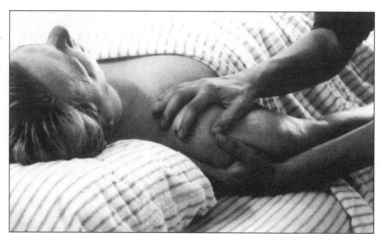

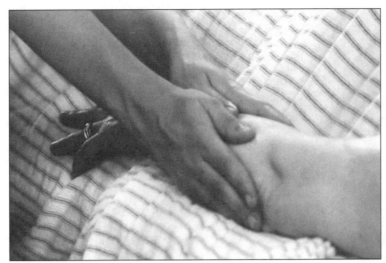

4 Pull your hands slowly back down the arm, over the wrist and the hand.

5 Sandwich the hand between yours for a moment, and then begin the gliding stroke again. Let your massage strokes resemble long refreshing waves covering the sand.

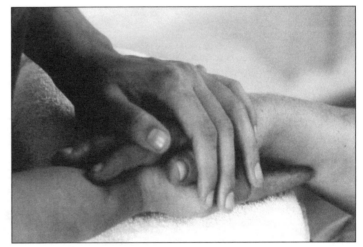

Kneading the Upper Arm

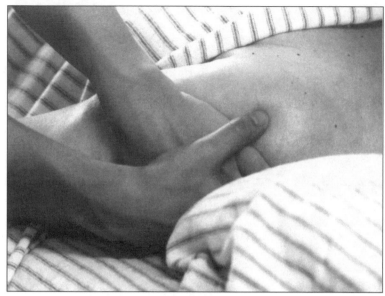

6 Stroke the upper arm and gather up the muscles here (biceps, triceps and deltoid). Squeeze and roll them between your hands. The arms and hands are packed with emotions, both loving and angry ones. Working here can awaken these feelings and memories, as well as feelings of strength and empowerment. As you work here, give this person the gift of your attentiveness. Embody the Shepherd's promise, "I will revive your drooping spirit!" (Psalm 23).

Stroking the Elbow

4 Bend the arm. Support the wrist with one hand while using the inside of your other arm to stroke back and forth, across the crease here. This stoke is very soothing; do it slowly.

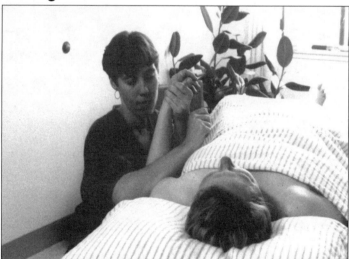

Stroking the Inside of the Arm

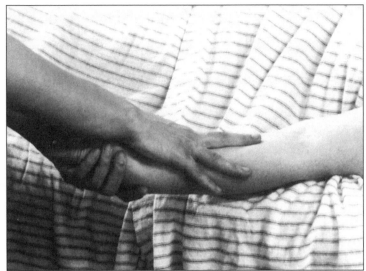

8 Rest the back of the arm on the table; support the back of the wrist as you stroke from the wrist to the top of the forearm and back down again. Do this stroke slowly and thoroughly with a medium amount of pressure. This prepares the arm for the following stroke.

Thumb Circling the Inner Arm

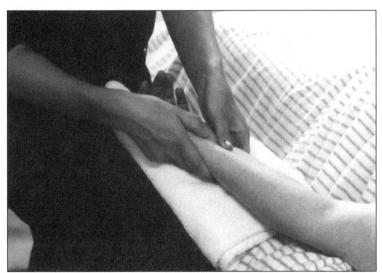

9 Cradle the arm near the wrist with both hands. Sink your thumbs down into the muscles and make small circular movements, thumbs moving in opposing directions. Work from the wrist up to the elbow; slide your hands back down the sides of the arm and repeat again. Be tender, be strong in your pressure as well as your presence. (Adjust your own body position as you need to, kneeling, sitting, standing, whatever enables you to work with the greatest amount of comfort, and will contribute to creating a sense of peace and simple intimacy between the two of you.)

Stroking the Outer Arm

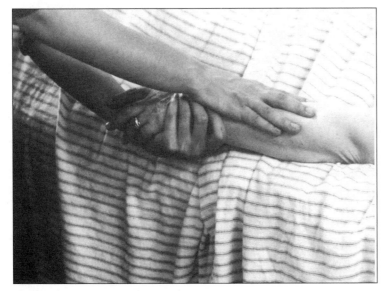

10 Turn the arm over, palm facing downward. Support the underside of the wrist with one hand; lean into the palm of your other hand as you press your fingers into the muscles and tendons here. This area welcomes firm pressure as these muscles are responsible for articulating many of the movements of the fingers.

Thumb Circling the Outer Arm

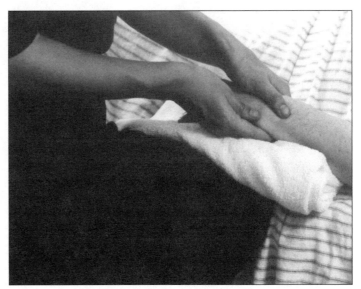

11 Support the arm by wrapping your fingers around the wrist. Do small circular movements with your thumbs, feeling into the spaces between the tendons. Release feelings of fatigue and restlessness that frequently settle in the arms and hands.

Restings

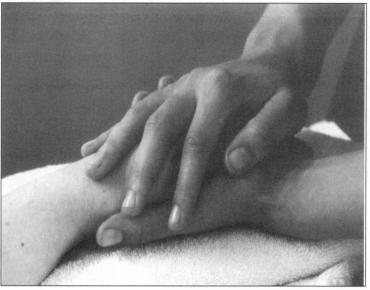

12 Nestle this hand between yours for a few moments; nothing to do and nothing to fix. Just a simple, honest benediction! "The Lord is my shepherd. I need nothing more" (Psalm 23).

(To continue on with the hand massage, please refer to the next chapter on "Hands.")

13 After completing the hand massage, repeat the gliding stroke, numbers 2-5, that you did at the beginning of the arm sequence. Place the arm beneath the sheet and brush from the shoulder down over the hand as a way of sealing in the peace. Repeat this sequence on the other arm.

Finishing/Draping

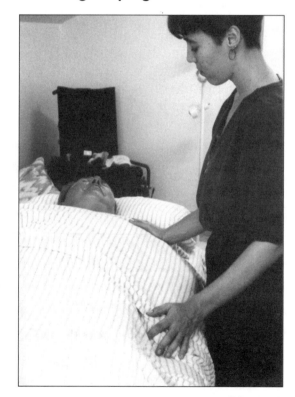

Bowing

Peace to you
Peace to all!

Hands

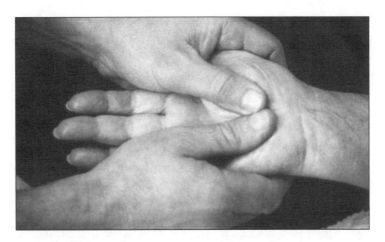

*H*uman hands are sensitive, expressive and articulate. Thousands of nerve endings blanket the palms of the hands and the tips of the fingers. This network of nerves allows the hands to respond accurately and immediately to temperature, pressure and texture. Hands have been called the "brain at the end of the arms," because they can accomplish the work ordered by the mind. Through our hands we have knowledge (as the Scholastics taught: "Nothing enters the mind except through the senses"). Through our hands we make connections with life — with plants, animals and humans; we enter the lives of others and affirm our own existence. Through our hands we make promises, we take oaths, we say prayers, we express our love and devotion, we extend ourselves in simple acts of kindness. Through our hands we make music and create masterpieces of art.

Like breath, hands are often taken for granted until something limits the ability to use them. Hands are personal and revealing. They can shout our nervousness, display our confidence and proffer our tenderness. They can shock us with their honesty and amaze us with their wisdom. Because our hands are so visible and accessible, we generally have fewer inhibitions about being touched by or touching another's hands; so the hand massage is a safe place to start practicing your massage skills. The hand massage is a simple but skillful way to acknowledge another's goodness and dignity. It is nonverbal therapy. It is a non invasive gesture that says, "I care."

Benefits of Hand Massage

◆ Relieves the hands and wrists of tiredness and stiffness. Aids circulation and warms cold hands.

◆ Helps to open up the flow of energy in the wrist, a key junction point where many of the arm's nerves, muscles, tendons and ligaments merge.

◆ Keeps the fingers and thumbs nimble. Relieves the aches and pains that come from arthritis and aging. Relaxes hands fatigued by hours of detailed work.

◆ Restores flexibility and range of motion in the joints, which in turn restores confidence and independence.

◆ Moisturizes the skin and keeps the hands soft and smooth.

◆ Heals both the hands and the heart. We all know that our hands can be instruments of violence and abuse. Anointing the hands through massage can awaken a sense of repentance and forgiveness; it can affirm one's commitment to living a vocation to care.

◆ Blesses and relaxes the whole person while caring for the hands.

Conditions, Precautions and Contraindications

◆ **Strains and Sprains:** The hands, particularly the wrists, are vulnerable to injuries resulting from overwork and overextension. In general, massage is not advised for sprains (injury causing inflammation and swelling to a ligament) or strains (injury causing inflammation and swelling to a muscle or tendon). When the swelling and inflammation have subsided, however, you may use whatever strokes feel good to your partner. The recovery time after a sprain can be greatly reduced with regular massage. Always remind the receiver to guide you concerning the appropriate amount of pressure. When in doubt, less is always better!

◆ **Arthritis** is an inflammation and swelling of the joints that can be very painful and can restrict the things we do with our hands. Never apply pressure or stroking to the immediate area if it is painful; however, gentle work in the area surrounding the inflammation can be very beneficial. Always honor whatever mobility the person might have, however limited it might be. Always work within their range of comfort. When the inflammation is reduced, slow, small micro movements to the fingers and/or the wrists, can be very helpful for increasing range of motion. Emotionally, this kind of care is also very therapeutic, as it helps to counteract a sense of uselessness and dependence.

◆ **Carpel Tunnel** is a constriction of the tendons, blood vessels and medial nerves around the carpals (wrist bones). This condition causes swelling, inflammation and acute pain. Massage is very beneficial for this condition but one needs to work very very gently. Never bend the wrist forward, backward or sideways. Try to keep the hand in its natural relaxed position while you are working with it.

◆ **Tendonitis** is an inflammation of the tendons in the hand. This can easily happen due to overuse. It is usually very painful and, as a general precaution, you do not massage a painful area. However, you can gently rest your hand over the area and let the warmth and comfort from your hands penetrate the condition. The hand will respond to this kind of holding in much the same way the body and spirit respond to a reassuring hug. The human connection and warm touch is healing for the hand.

The Physical Anatomy of the Hands

Twenty-seven bones and fourteen joints form the framework for each hand's muscles, veins, arteries and thousands of nerve endings.

Each hand contains:

- ◆ 8 wrist bones
   (carpal bones)
- ◆ 5 hand bones
   (metacarparal bones)
- ◆ 14 finger bones
   (phalanges)

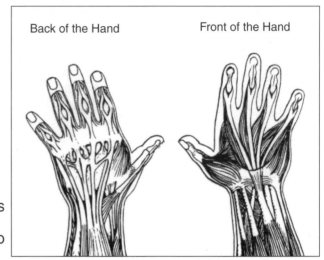

Back of the Hand   Front of the Hand

Each finger consists of three small bones except for the thumb, which has two bones. The places were the bones meet are called joints, and in the case of the hand, these joints are called knuckles.

Muscles

The intricate movements of the fingers and thumbs are facilitated by tendons which attach to the muscles in the forearms. For this reason, it is always a good idea to include a little massage to the arms when giving a hand massage. Over the bony framework, there are many muscles that spread out over the hand enabling it to open and close, to grasp and let go, to work and to rest.

Arteries and Veins

Arteries and veins which carry the life blood and oxygen to and from these "extensions of the heart" flow beneath the surface of the soft tissue.

Carpal Ligament

Finally, holding this amazing framework and network in place, there is a bracelet-like ligament that wraps around the wrist, called the carpal ligament.

Position

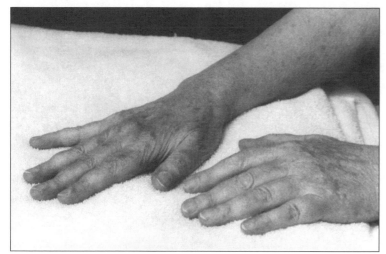

Chair

Sit to the side, facing the receiver. Place a pillow across both of your laps. Cover the pillow with a soft towel. Rest the receiver's hand on the pillow.

Hospital bed

If appropriate, you can sit on the side of the bed facing the patient. Otherwise, sit on a chair or stool next to the bed; lower the guard rail and the bed so you can work comfortably and without straining your back. You can place a small pil-

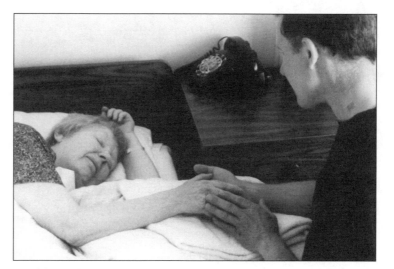

low beneath the patient's forearm and hand to elevate it a little and provide support.

Equipment and Environment

◆ pillow and towels

◆ lotion or oil

◆ tape recorder and quiet, pleasant music, if desired

◆ an appropriate symbol reflecting the goodness and beauty of life: a flower,

a candle, favorite picture, memento from a special person or place

Assessment

Spend a couple of minutes gathering whatever personal information is necessary from your partner concerning his or her general health and the condition of the hands and arms at this time. This will help you to work more intelligently and com-passionately. It will also help them to relax, knowing that you are aware of any conditions that might be causing them some difficulty.

The Massage Sequence

I make holy whatever I touch or am touched by.
— Walt Whitman

Centering

1 Be sure that both you and your partner are comfortable. Then, before touching, take a couple of minutes to be quiet and centered together. Become aware of yourself, and what you are about to do. Adjust your posture to be sure you are at ease. Notice your hands and be grateful for these simple gifts of love and mercy. Make an intention that this time of caring through touch will be a time of blessing for both of you.

Rub your hands together to bring a feeling of warmth into them. Then rest your hands over your heart for a moment and remind yourself that massage, the art of anointing and blessing, is heart work, and not hard work!

2 Apply lotion or oil to your hands and begin to become acquainted with this hand. Take your time spreading the lotion on the hand and up into the forearm (provided the clothing will allow for this).

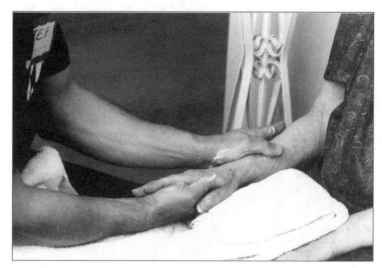

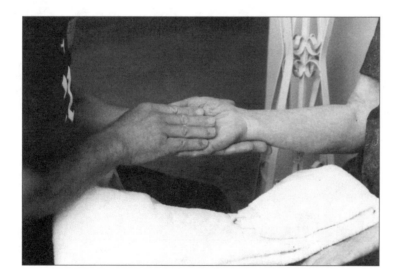

3 As you massage, notice the little things that make this hand unique – the lines and creases running over the palm of the hand, the texture of the skin, its shape. Watch your own hands moving and creating a dance of friendship.

Wrist

4 Support your partner's hand in both of yours. Begin to make small circular movements with the balls of your thumbs across the back of the wrist. Work slowly and carefully into all the little spaces.

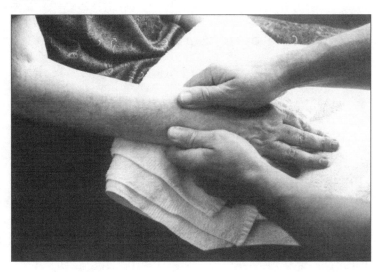

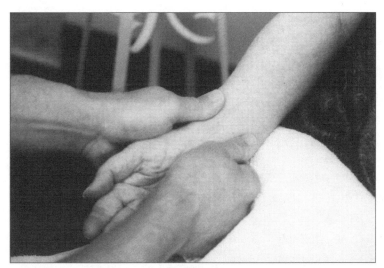

5 Turn the hand over and thumb circle back and forth across the inside of the wrist and a little ways up into the forearm. This is a very important area to massage because it is the key juncture point for many nerves, muscles, and tendons that stream down the arm and into the hand. Glide your fingers around the "knobs" or the bony protrusions on either side of the wrist. You can never spend too much time massaging this overused joint. Massage will help to relieve stiffness and restore flexibility.

Back of the Hand and Thumb Stroking

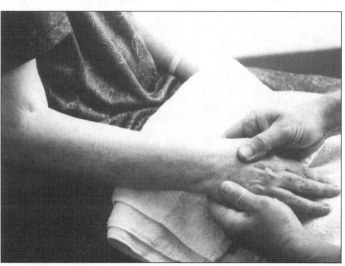

6 Turn the hand over so the palm is facing down. Support the palm side of the hand with your fingers. Massage the back of the hand by thumb circling from the base of the fingers to the wrist and into the forearm. Notice the hand bones (metacarpals) rippling under your thumbs as you massage over them. This is detailed work, much as an artist might work in softening and shaping a piece of clay. Be sure to remain relaxed in your own hands. Let your hands be an extension of your heart.

Rotating the Hand

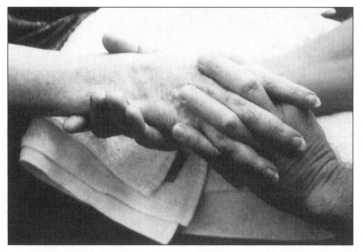

7 Support the forearm and wrist by holding it loosely in the palm of your hand. Interlace your fingers with the receiver's and carefully rotate the hand several times in one direction, and then in the other. Respect the range of motion here. Work gently and precisely.

Bending the Wrist

8 Maintain the same hand position as before. Slowly bend the hand backwards and forwards, flexing and extending the hand and wrist. Observe any signs of resistance, and never push beyond what feels comfortable If there has been an injury to the wrist, or any sign of inflammation, you will want to pass over this stroke.

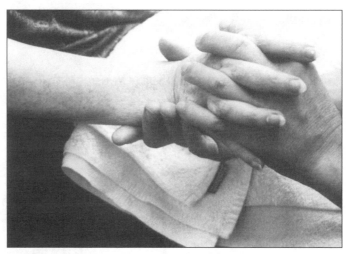

Rest

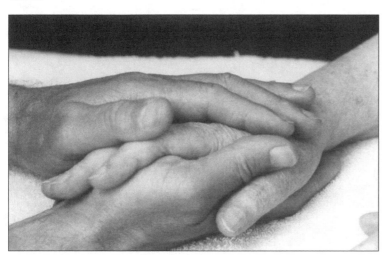

9 Support the person's hand in both of yours; take a moment to appreciate this quiet contact. Relax your shoulders, relax your breathing. Let go of any effort to get it "right," and instead enjoy a moment of doing nothing at all.

Finger Massage

10 Grasp the base of the little finger between your thumb and index finger. Slide your fingers back towards their fingertip by gently and slowly rotating the finger. Imagine the tension in this person's fingers dissolving as you move from finger to finger.

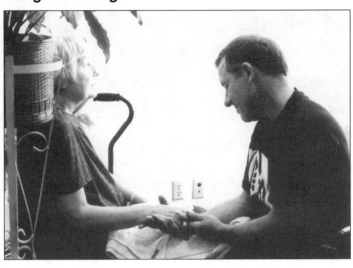

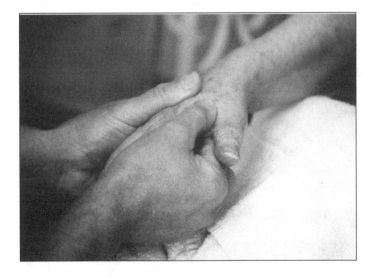

11 Massage well into the base of the thumb, and into the webbing between the thumb and index finger. This area is often quite sensitive and sore, so watch the receiver's face for any signs of discomfort from your pressure.

Brushing the Palm

12 Turn the hand over so the palm is facing upward and cradle the back of the person's hand in yours. Use the side of your hand to brush over the palm and out to the edges of the fingers. Observe the way in which the lines crisscross back and forth like a road map here, telling and foretelling this life's journey.

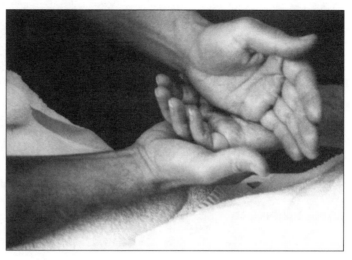

Kneading the Palm

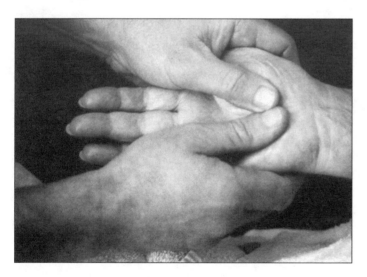

13 Soften the fleshy part of the palm by kneading it slowly with your thumbs. Inch your way along like a caterpillar here, pressing carefully into the spaces between the hand bones, working from the heel of the hand to the base of the fingers.

Circling the Palm

14 Cradle the back of the person's hand in one of yours: make a soft fist with your other hand and slowly circle the palm. Imagine you are shaping the hand into a warm nest where kindness and compassion can rest.

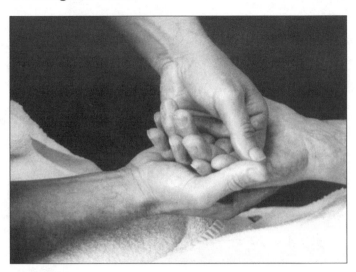

Resting

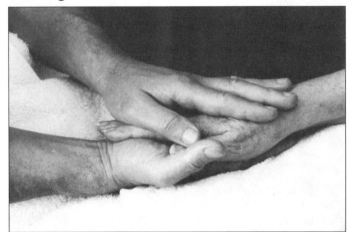

15 Rest the hand, palm facing down. Gently brush hand over hand from the forearm to the fingertips. Then cradle the receiver's hand in yours. Hold this contact for a few seconds and seal in the warmth and trust that have been generated between the two of you.

16 Then slowly let your hands slip away,

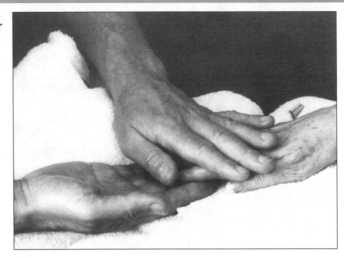

17 Gently shake out your own hands and arms; relax your neck and shoulders; then, take the towel and wipe off any access oil or lotion from the person's hand and return it to the lap or the bed.

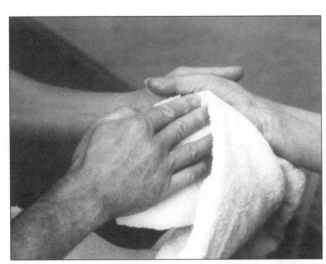

18 Move to the other hand and repeat the same sequence.

Bowing

Peace to you
Peace to all!

Chest and Abdomen

*T*here is a normal human attitude and animal reflex that tries to hide and protect the body's underside. The belly and the breasts are often the most vulnerable, scarred, abandoned and abused parts of the body. There is an ambivalence in our experience of our belly and chest. On the one hand it can be a sensual and private experience and on the other it can be an experience of shame, isolation and self-hatred. Massage as anointing offers the potential for reclaiming the body in the image of the Creator.

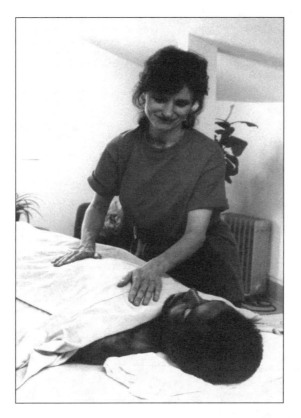

During massage, as the shoulders and chest muscles relax and the breath deepens, people often sigh with relief as they let go of years of fear and hurt, of isolation, loneliness and shame, and open to the possibilities of forgiveness and intimacy once again.

Benefits of Chest and Abdomen Massage

◆ Relaxes the chest muscles and increases the flexibility of the ribs, thus deepening the breathing which is essential for overall relaxation and well-being.

◆ Opens the chest muscles and creates a sense of expansiveness throughout the chest, shoulders and upper back.

◆ Relieves congestion and muscle tension and soreness due to coughing, colds, flu and allergies.

◆ Enhances the circulation of blood and oxygen which in turn will raise the body's temperature, lower the heart rate and stabilize blood pressure.

◆ Aids in pumping the lymph more efficiently through the body, thus helping to eliminate the body toxins through the lymph system; this will strengthen the body's immune system.

◆ Soothes and cleanses the organs of digestion and elimination and relieves constipation and gas.

◆ Softens and loosens adhesions from surgeries and restores movement and flexibility to the scarred areas.

◆ Eases and releases feelings of sadness and disappointment that often settle around the heart. Massage can awaken feelings of joy, love and care.

◆ Helps "untie" the knots and cramps we so frequently feel in our bellies when we are worried or afraid; it can awaken feelings of strength and vitality.

◆ Helps to create a more positive self-image, particularly if the body has been marred through surgery, or has been ridiculed or violated in any way.

◆ Helps to draw us forth from a place of isolation and into a relationship with ourselves, the world and with God.

◆ Brings a healing and sacred silence into the body and the mind.

◆ Helps the person to feel nurtured, loved and cherished.

Conditions, Precautions and Modifications

◆ For many reasons people feel very protective of this part of the body. Be attentive to the person's sense of vulnerability and their need for privacy. Take care in the way you drape them. Some women may feel vulnerable if their breasts are exposed. If this is so, place a soft towel over the breasts while you massage the abdomen.

◆ Inquire about recent surgeries such as heart or gall bladder, mastectomy or hysterectomy. Never massage or apply pressure over a fresh incision or recent scar. However, it is very healing to make gentle contact by simply resting you hands over a recent wound or incision, provided it is protected with a bandage. This should always be talked over with the person beforehand. We all tend to be very vulnerable and protective of our hurts, physical or emotional. Asking permission to touch the part of the body that is especially wounded, can be very healing in and of itself.

◆ If a person tends to be ticklish, be sensitive to your pressure. The more slowly you massage, the more likely they will be able to relax and trust you. If the area of the chest is sensitive and tender, massage very gently and slowly.

◆ Never massage over the nipples.

◆ Be sensitive to menstrual cramping and bloating.

◆ Sometimes massage can be very soothing for an upset stomach. At other times the stomach may be very sensitive to touch. This is a time when the warmth that is generated through gentle holding can be very healing. You may want to elevate the head if the person is lying down.

◆ Do not massage over the area of a cancer. Attentive resting of the hands over or near the area can be very therapeutic and healing.

◆ Whatever the condition – physical, emotional or spiritual – meet the person who is carrying this condition with kindness and compassion.

The Physical Anatomy of the Chest and Abdomen

The torso or trunk of the body is divided into two halves intersecting at the diaphragm. The first half which we call the chest, begins at the shoulders and extends through the diaphragm, and the second half, called the abdomen, begins at the diaphragm and extends to the pubic bone.

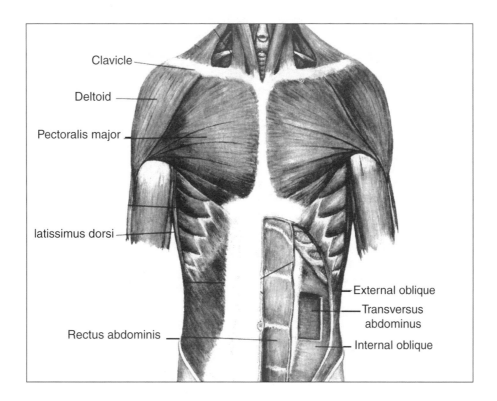

Bones of the Upper Torso

The **shoulder girdle** is made up of the collarbones (clavicle) in front, and the shoulder blades (scapula) in back.

Twelve sets of ribs attach to the breastbone (sternum) in front, and the twelve thoracic vertebrae in the back This "rib cage" is a flexible cave-like structure that protects the heart and supports the movement of the lungs.

The sternum (breastbone) is a strong bone that adds additional protection for the heart.

Muscles of the Upper Torso

The **pectorals** (pectoralis major) overlie the upper portion of the rib cage and attach to the top of the arm. They help draw the arms together.

Two layers of small **intercostal muscles** knit the rib bones together. These muscles help to open and lift the ribs as the lungs expand with the intake of fresh air, and help the ribs to draw in and descend as old air is expelled.

The **diaphragm** is a strong sheath of muscle attached to the bottom of the ribs and stretches around to the backbone. This dome-shaped muscle is responsible for the depth to which we can breathe, laugh and sigh, and is therefore often referred to as the muscle that is key to both our physical and emotional energy. It also serves as a passageway for other important sources of energy. Openings in the diaphragm allow the major blood vessels to carry blood to and from the lower body, and also make it possible for the esophagus to pass food to the stomach.

Organs in the Upper Torso

Within this beautifully crafted cave-like frame reside the two organs that pump life, in the form of air and blood, throughout the body.

The **hear**t nestles between the two lobes of the lungs and behind the breastbone (sternum). In an average adult the heart will weigh about 10-11 ounces, and will pump approximately 1,250 gallons of blood a day throughout every part of the body.

The **lungs** are soft, light and spongy, resembling honeycombs. In the average adult, each lung can hold approximately 3 quarts of precious air with every breath.

The heart and the lungs act as team, channeling healing rivers of energy throughout the body.

Bones of the Lower Torso

The **pelvic girdle** consists of two identical fan-like halves that connect in the back to the sacrum, and are framed on either side by the hips. Each half is made up of three bones which are fused together. The pelvis holds the digestive and reproductive organs, creates a passageway for the birth canal and for the elimination of waste materials from the digestive processes.

Muscles of the Lower Torso

Four layers of strong and uniquely crafted muscles support the pelvic structure and its corresponding internal organs.

The **transversus abdominis** is the deepest of the three muscles. The fibers of this muscle extend across the abdominal area and act like a girdle, securely holding the organic contents of the abdomen.

The **external and internal obliques** are muscles that make up the second and third layers. These flat muscles lie in a diagonal fashion across the abdomen and the lower part of the ribs. They are the muscles that help form the sides of the body, along with the back's latissimus dorsi muscles.

The **rectus abdominus** is the top-most muscle that extends vertically from the base of the rib cage and the diaphragm down to the pubic bone. This muscle, along with help from the back muscles, allows the torso to bend in half.

Organs in the Lower Torso

The abdominal muscles support the pelvic structure and protect the organs of digestion: stomach, liver, intestines, gall bladder and spleen; the organs of elimination: kidneys, bladder, colon and rectum; and the reproductive organs. A Tantric song proclaims the miracle of the body like this: "Here in this body are the sacred rivers: here are the sun and moon, as well as all the pilgrimage places. I have not encountered another temple as blissful as my own body."

Preparations for Massaging Chest and Abdomen

Position

Massage on the front of the body is best given by having the person lie on a flat surface that is both firm and comfortable. A bed is usually not an appropriate place for a massage, because it is too wide, and not firm enough. If you work on a table that is about waist-to-thigh-high you will be able to lean your body's weight into your hands and arms in a comfortable and confident way. If working at a table is not convenient, the massage can be given on a floor. Use a 2-3 inch foam mat or a sleeping bag for padding. Cover the mat with soft flannel sheets.

Equipment and Environment

◆ pillows. Place a bed pillow under the knees to help release tension in the low back muscles and the abdomen. Keep a few extra pillows handy for additional comfort and support.

◆ towels. Place a folded towel under the head to release holding in the neck and throat. Large heavy bath towels can also be used to provide extra warmth if your partner gets chilly during the massage.

◆ tape recorder and relaxing music, if desired.

◆ oil or lotion. It's nice to have these at room temperature or even a little warmer. You may want to warm the oil by placing the container in hot water or in front of a heater.

◆ space. Take special care to arrange the room so that it is welcoming, warm and safe, and that a sense of the sacred is evident. Privacy, quiet and cleanliness are important for relaxation and reflection.

Assessment

If you are going to massage the chest and abdomen apart from the rest of the body, you will want to spend a few minutes gathering information that will help you be more attentive to your partner's needs and compassionate about his or her vulnerability.

Inquire about your partner's health. If you know the person well, you might ask how things are going in general. Be a good listener.

Many people, both men and women, at first will feel a bit apprehensive and shy about removing their clothes and having their breasts and belly exposed and touched unless it is by someone they trust. Let your partner know that should they begin to feel uncomfortable or afraid at any time during the massage they shouldn't hesitate to let you know, and together you can decide how best to continue. Remind them that they can remove or leave on whatever amount of clothing will make them feel most comfortable and safe.

Leave the room while the person is undressing and getting onto the table.

The Massage Sequence

I will lay down my life for my friends.
— Jesus

Centering

1 Stand at the side of the table. Take a moment to clear your mind of any negative or judgmental thoughts, or any tendencies to fix or change this person. Reconnect with the presence of God, breathing and living in you. Feel grounded and rooted in your intention to be present in a healing way to this person.

Laying on of Hands

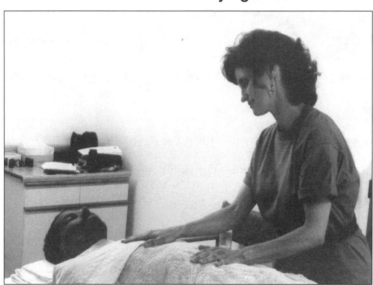

2 Let your hands slowly and quietly come to rest over the sheet like a blessing on the body, one over the belly, the other over the chest. See and feel your partner's breathing as if you were a mother or a father watching a new-born child breathe. Linger here for a few seconds and let the trust begin to be established between the two of you.

Drawing back the Sheet and Applying Oil

3 Remove your hands and careful-ly draw the sheet down to just below the navel. Return your hands to the belly and the heart as a gesture of loving protection. Make sure that every part of your hand (and mind), is touching them with confidence and love. Slowly withdraw your hands and walk to the head of the table. Apply oil to your hands and arms.

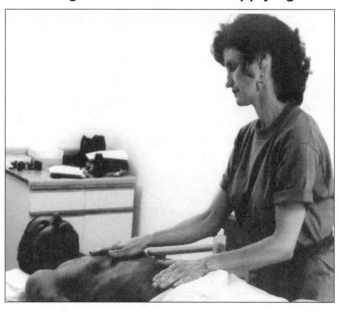

Gliding Stroke

4 In order to maintain good leverage for this gliding stroke, place one foot in front of the other. Let both of your hands come to rest on the upper body.

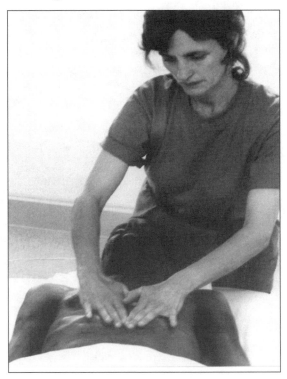

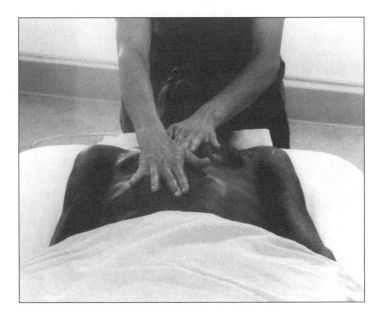

5 Lean forward over your front foot as you slowly slide your hands over the breastbone, the abdomen and down to the waist.

137

6 Slide your hands across the abdomen to the sides of the waist.

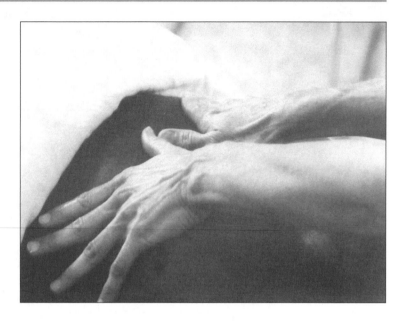

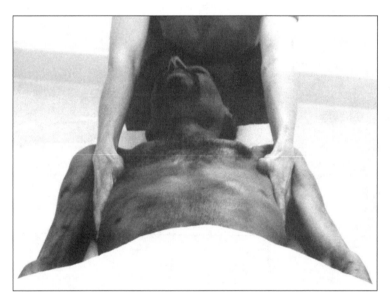

7 Bend your back knee and lean back as you slowly pull your hands up the sides of the body and over the shoulders.

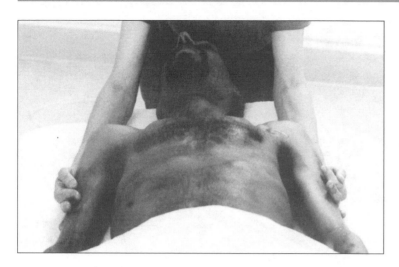

8 Slide your hands down onto the upper arms, cradling the body; then stroke up the arms and over the shoulders.

9 Return your hands to the upper chest. Repeat this gliding stroke three or four times, varying your pressure as you massage.

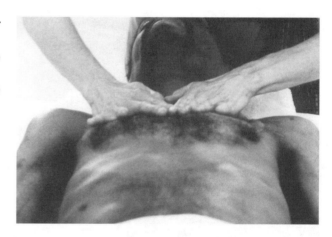

Finger Circling on the Chest

10 Lay the fingers of both hands on the upper chest beneath the collarbones. Keep the fingers close together as you rotate them in small circles. Press gently but firmly as you work thoroughly over the upper chest and into the areas just in front of the armpits.

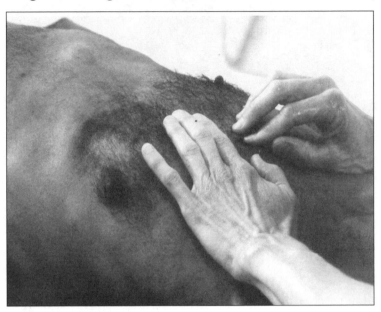

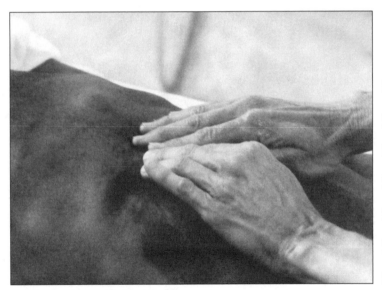

1 Move carefully down along the sternum keeping your rhythm steady and your pressure gentle as this area in front of the heart can be very tender. Repeat this two or three times. Conclude with steps 6-9 of the sequence. When this stroke is performed slowly and carefully, it can have a profound therapeutic effect on the person's breathing.

Blessing

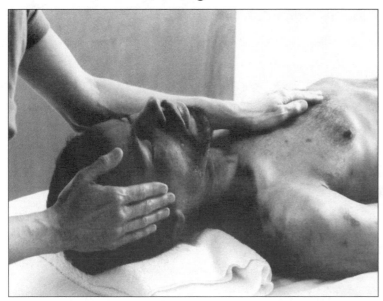

12 Place one hand against the side of the head. Rest your other hand quietly over the heart. Offer this person your own heart through your hands.

*To offer one's heart is
the greatest gift of all.*
— Anonymous

Side Abdominal Stroking

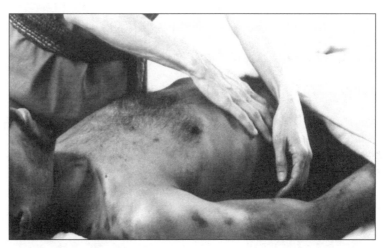

13 Step to the side of the table. Reach across and place both hands on the side of the abdomen opposite you, just below the waist. Separate your feet and drop down into your own center as you begin to pull one hand slowly up and in towards the navel. As this hand arrives at the center, the other hand begins at the side and moves toward the center of the body. Your hands will create a lovely kind of dance here if you maintain a slow, steady and rhythmic pace, hands alternating and overlapping. Carry this wave-like stroking up the side of the abdomen and the rib cage, ending just beneath the breast, and then stroke back down again. Never be in a hurry. These strokes will help to soften the abdomen and the diaphragm muscles and prepare them for the kneading strokes.

Kneading the Abdomen

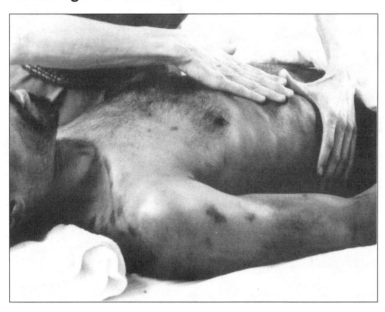

14 Place both hands on the side of the abdomen opposite you, just below the waist (external oblique muscle). Alternately use the hands to pull, lift and gently squeeze the muscles between the thumb and fingers. Knead rhythmically hand over hand between the top of the pelvis and the bottom of the rib cage. Remain aware of your own body, letting your hips gently move and swing in rhythm with your hands. Massage is creative work, it's being willing to be shaped beyond one's imagination into a beautiful body, a body that embodies the Christ.

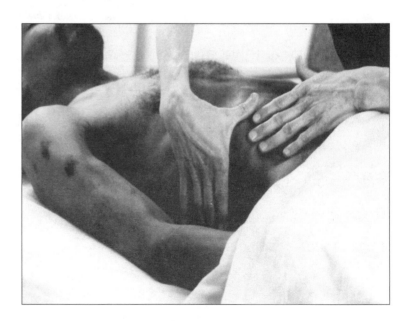

Rest!

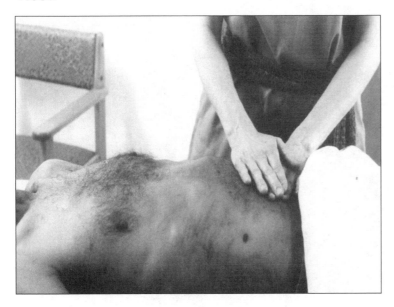

15 Rest your hands over the navel. Relax your shoulders, and your arms; hold effortlessly, hold freely. Receive this life into your hands like a mother receives her baby. Be filled with wonder and thankfulness that you can touch this precious life.

Circling the Abdomen

16 Begin to move your hands in a clockwise circle around the immediate area of the navel. Let the upper hand propel and guide the under hand; let your whole body turn with your hands. The pelvis, hips and knees will follow the wheel-like turning of your hands. This slow, thoughtful, and firm stroking can evoke a vibrant feeling of calm and relaxation.

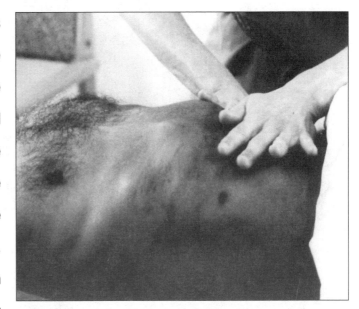

17 Let the circle open up and grow steadily wider, higher and deeper as your hands cover the entire area of the abdomen.

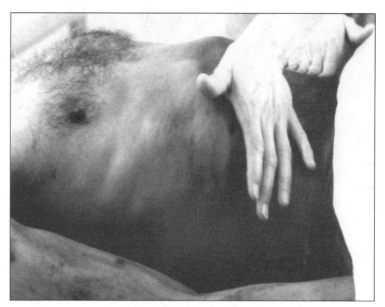

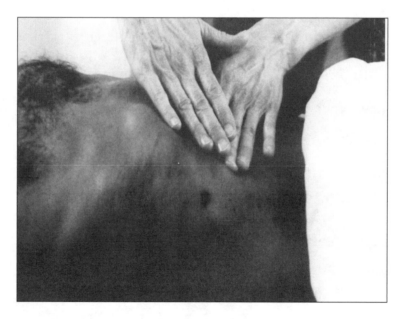

18 Let the tips of your fingers sink carefully into the small space at the base of the breastbone, the second largest collection of nerves in the body. Move on down the side of the abdomen nearest you, across the lower part of the abdomen just below the navel and up the opposite side. Maintain an awareness of your own breathing being present but not overpowering as you guard and anoint the center of power and mercy.

19 Now rest your hands, one upon the other, on the belly. Be touched by the effortless rising and falling of the breathing beneath your hands; be in wonder at this body of Christ.

Holding the Center

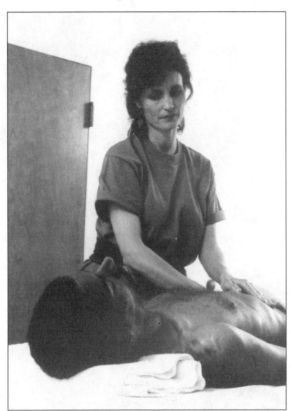

Gliding Stroke

20 Slowly withdraw your hands from the belly. Walk back to the head of the table, and conclude with several of the long gliding strokes, strokes that will include the shoulders and the neck as well. Repeat two or three times.

Resting and Blessing

21 Let your hands rest over the upper chest.

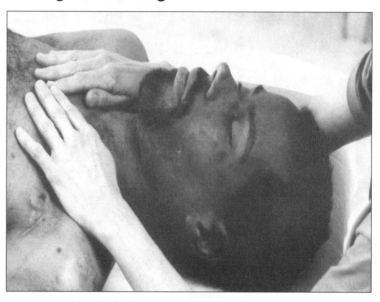

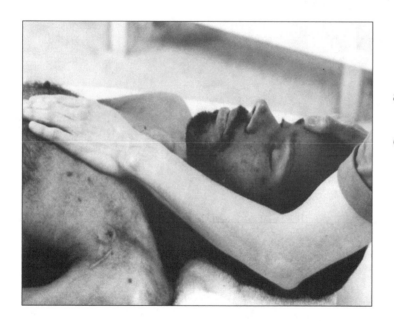

22 Rest one hand on the heart and the other alongside the head.

Give of your hands to serve and your hearts to love.
– Mother Teresa

Slowly remove your hands.

Draping

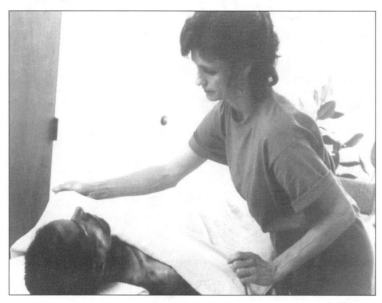

23 Return to the side of the table and carefully cover the person with the sheet. Treat the sheet with the same reverence that you have given to the body; it is an extension of this person.

24 Let your hands settle one last time over the abdomen and chest. Remove your hands; bring them together in the prayer pose.

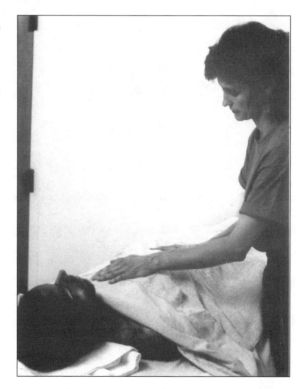

Bowing

Peace to you
Peace to all!

Neck and Shoulders

God is my shepherd,
He carries me upon his shoulders.
I wrap my arms around his neck;
he carries me to where the grass is green,
to where the waters are still.
I drink and I am filled with life.
— Psalm 23

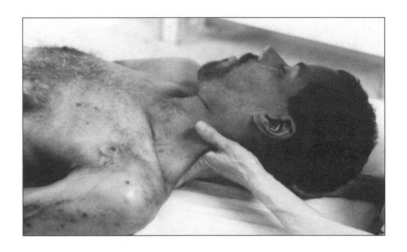

The neck is like a channel, a passageway that connects the mind and the body, thought and action, imagination and communication, spirituality and physicality. Beginning with the very top vertebra, the "atlas," the neck is there to channel the mind's thoughts and ideas into the body's tissues, where the body will refine them and shape them into beautiful and wise actions. The neck can nod in affirmation or turn to say "no"; it can bow in homage or bend in shame; it can lift in exhilaration or freeze in haughtiness; it can embrace all perspectives or become rigid with resistance. There is always need for a neck massage, reassurance that it may continue to be "a channel of peace."

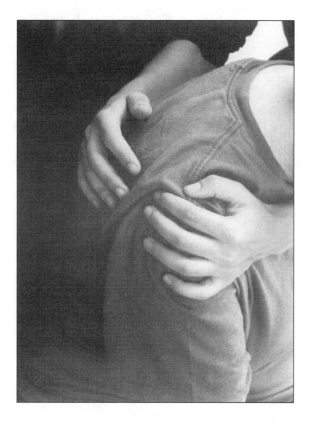

The shoulders are like scales that weigh what the arms bring from the heart to the world. The way the arms hang in the balance reflects the energy it takes to "shoulder responsibility" and to "be supportive." Shoulders are an easy part of the anatomy to read; they open with pride, round with protective-ness, slump with fatigue. They carry not only the weight of the head, but also the weight of thoughts, worries, plans and dreams.

Benefits of Neck and Shoulder Massage

◆ Relieves tension-related headaches and stiffness in the neck caused in part by stress in the scalp, poor posture, and lack of movement and exercise.

◆ Improves circulation to the head and to the arms and hands by stimulating the flow of blood through tightly held neck and shoulder muscles, and by stretching and relaxing the muscle tissues.

◆ Increases range of motion in the neck and shoulder muscles.

◆ Relieves muscular pain and soreness in the shoulders from repetitively using the neck, shoulder, arm and hand muscles, as in a sport such as tennis or in work-related activities such as computer work, sewing, assembly line work and playing musical instruments.

◆ Causes shoulders and arms to feel more mobile, and allows them to swing more freely, and more playfully.

◆ Eases emotional pain and helps a person feel less burdened, and more appreciated.

Conditions, Precautions and Modifications

◆ If a person has had injuries to the areas of the neck and shoulders that have resulted in limited range of motion or chronic pain, be sensitive to the amount of pressure you apply here. The causes of limitation may include trauma from a car accident, such as whiplash (cervical sprain); or from arthritis, osteoporosis or dowager's hump. Holding and very gentle stretching and pressing can be very helpful in these situations.

◆ Even though the neck and shoulders are thought to be the most stressed areas of the body, this does not give you permission to work hard or dig into the muscles here. Quite the contrary! Because it is a major connecting point between the head and torso and because it is a passageway for the nerves to move from the head into the rest of the body, gentleness and sensitivity are very important when massaging the neck and shoulders.

◆ A painful burning sensation in the area of the shoulder and upper arm could indicate bursitis, and even the slightest amount of stroking will increase the sensation. Gentle holding over the area will be most helpful.

◆ Pinched nerves due to muscle constriction is a common condition of the neck. This will usually manifest as a shooting kind of pain in this area. Massage can be done, but be attentive to the person's comfort.

The Physical Anatomy of the Neck and Shoulders

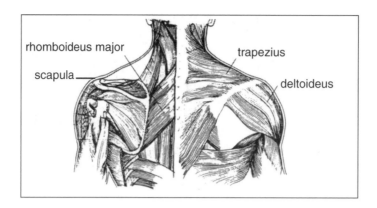

Neck Bones

The neck is made up of seven cervical vertebrae that connect the head with the rest of the body. The topmost vertebra is called the atlas, the name of the Greek titan who was destined to support the weight of the world on his shoulders. Many people today feel that the preoccupations of their mind are as weighty as the world. There is one bone on the front side of the neck, the hyoid bone, to which the muscles here are connected.

Shoulder Bones

The shoulder girdle consists of two bones:

> the **clavicle** (collarbones), extending from the center of the neck just below the throat out to the shoulder

> the **scapulae** (shoulderblades), triangular wing-shaped bones on either side of the spine

The clavicle joins the scapula at about the place where a shoulder strap of a purse or bag might rest. The head or "ball" of the humerus (upper arm) fits snugly into the concave socket of the scapula. This ball-and-socket joint gives the arm its range of motion.

Neck Muscles

The upper portion of the **trapezius** begins at the base of the skull and covers the back of the neck. They are often times called the "yes" muscle because they help stabilize the head when it is bent forward.

The **sternoclydomastoid muscles** attach to the mastoid bone behind the ear and to the top of the sternum (breastbone) and the clavicle (collarbone). They help turn the head from side to side, and are sometimes referred to as our "no" muscles.

Shoulder Muscles

The **trapezius,** one of the most graceful and troublesome muscles of the body, is the predominant muscle that benefits from neck and shoulder massage. This muscle begins beneath the base of the skull and supports the head. It flows down the back of the neck, spills out over the shoulders, and spreads into the middle of the back in a v-shaped manner.

The **rhomboids,** which lie underneath the trapezius, are attached to the inner edge of the scapulae and the spine. This is a place where tension frequently hides out.

Other muscles included in this sequence are the **deltoids** that wrap around the tops of the shoulders; the **biceps** which lie over the front of the upper arm, enabling the arm to draw things towards the shoulders; and the **triceps** which lie along the back of the upper arm, making it possible to lower the arm.

Preparations for Giving a Neck and Shoulder Massage from a Table Position

Position

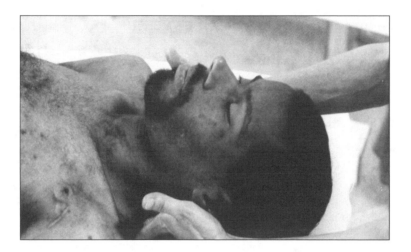

Giving a neck and shoulder massage to someone who is lying down is quite a bit different from massaging this area with the receiver seated in a chair.

In the following sequence the person would lie on his or her back on a flat surface, preferably a table that is about thigh or waist-high. If the table is not a professional massage table, you will want to cover it with a 2-3 inch foam pad, which in turn will be covered by a soft sheet. If a table is not available, you may put a foam mat on the floor and follow the same sequence. Working on the floor, however, requires a good deal of flexibility on the part of the giver, particularly in the hips, knees and back. Giving a massage on a bed is usually not advisable due to the softness of the mattress and the width of the bed.

Equipment and Environment

◆ table

◆ foam pad or folded blankets

◆ sheets. Soft flannel sheets are perfect, a fitted one for the foam pad, and another for warmth and cover. It is always a good idea to have a light blanket or several large towels close by in case the recipient get chilly.

◆ pillows. Place a pillow, the size of a bed pillow, under the knees; this will help relax the lower back and deepen the breathing. Since you will be massaging the neck and shoulders, there is usually no need for another pillow or towel under the head.

◆ tape recorder and relaxing music, if desired.

Assessment

Take a couple of minutes before you begin the massage to inquire how your partner is feeling. Remember to ask about any previous injuries in the areas of their neck and shoulders, such as sports injuries or whiplashes. Caring through touch begins in the attentive and receptive way we listen not only with our hands, but with our ears and our hearts to what the other person has to tell us.

The Massage Sequence

Prosper the work of your hands, Lord.

– Psalm 138

Centering

1 Stand at the head of the table. Quietly rest your hands on either side of the head. Feel rooted like a tree and centered as a mountain in your own body. Both are very significant Christian symbols that signify life and faith. Quietly rest your hands

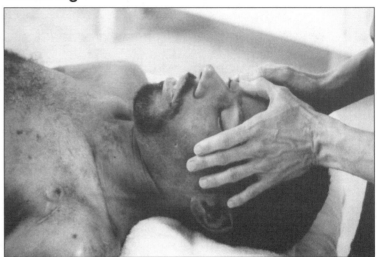

on either side of the head and see this person through the eyes of your heart.

Rocking the Head

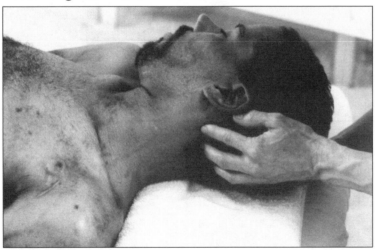

2 Cup the palms of your hands beneath the head and rock the head slowly from side to side. Rocking the head in this manner gently stretches the neck and tends to quickly dissolve negative feelings such as fear, frustration and anger.

Encourage your partner to soften the jaw, relax the tongue and take some deeper breaths. Slowly bring the head to a rest and withdraw your hands.

Gliding Stroke

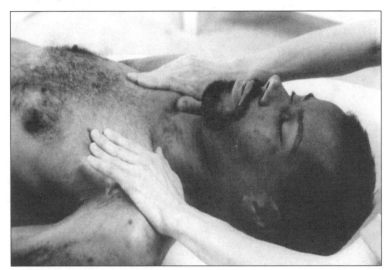

3 Apply a small amount of oil to your hands. Place the palms of your hands over the shoulders on either side of the neck.

4 Slowly sweep your hands out across the shoulder muscles;

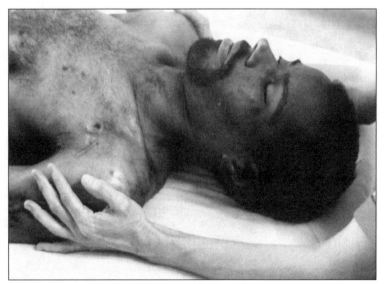

5 turn them so they curve around and slide under the shoulders,

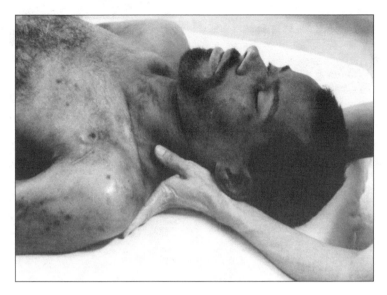

6 and come together at the back of the neck. Give a gentle stretch to the neck by slowly pulling your fingers back towards the occipital ridge – the boney landmarks at the base of the skull.

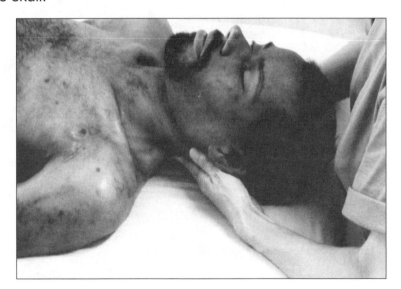

Cradling the Head

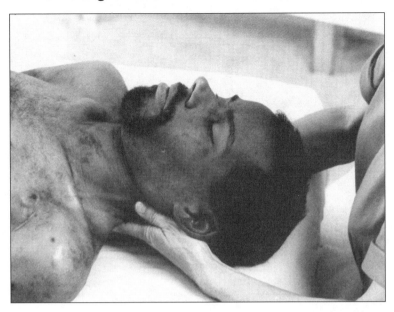

7 Pause and cradle the head for a moment; then slip your fingers out from either side of the neck. (Do not pull them up the back of the head and through the hair as this can pull the hair and feel uncomfortable.) Repeat the gliding stroke three or four times.

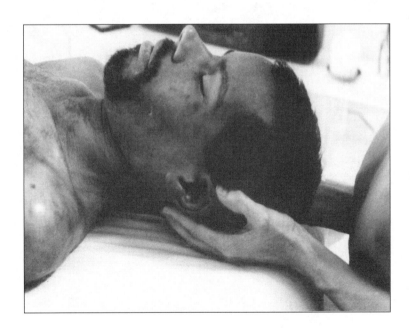

Kneading the Shoulders

8 Slip your fingers down behind the back of the shoulders and rest your thumbs on top.

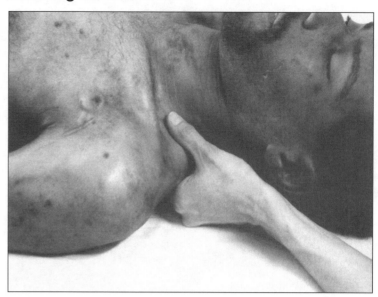

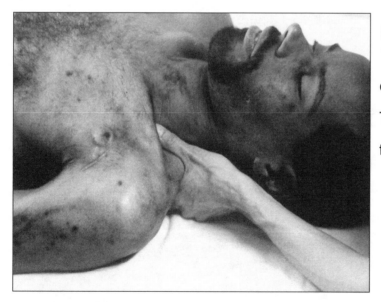

9 Squeeze deeply and slowly into and out of the muscles on top and beneath the shoulders. Take care not to press down on the collar bone (clavicle).

Neck Stroking

10 With one hand on either side of the neck stroke upwards from the top of the shoulders to the base of the head with alternate hands. Let your movements be slow, strong and graceful. If you shift the weight of your own body a little from left to right while stroking, you will create a slight rocking

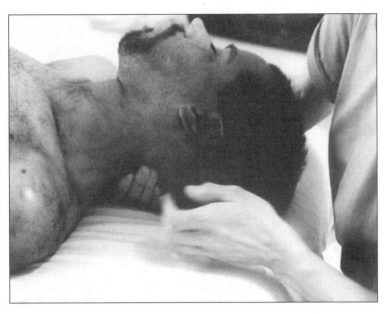

motion of the head. This will help facilitate the release of tightness in the neck muscles.

Neck and Shoulder Stroking

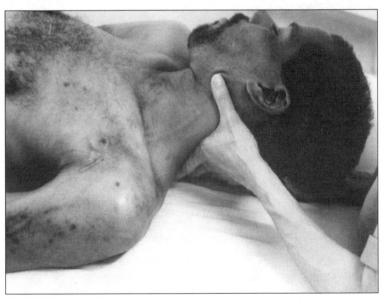

11 Turn the head to one side and let it rest in the palm of your hand. Position your hand so the side of the neck rests between your thumb and fingers. Stroke down the neck.

12 Stroke out across the top of the shoulder.

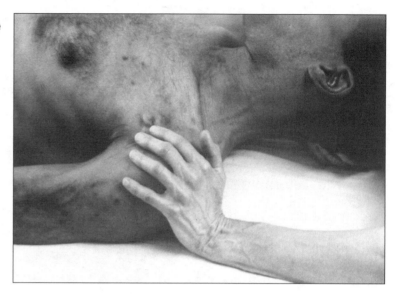

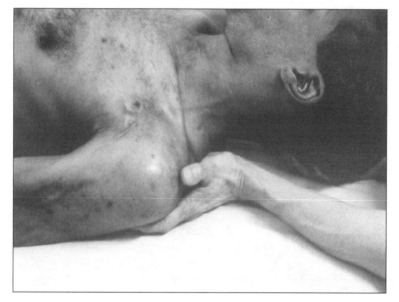

13 Sweep your hand around and behind the shoulder and up the side of the neck. Repeat this graceful sweeping stroke several times. Turn the head slowly to the other side and repeat numbers 11-13.

Resting

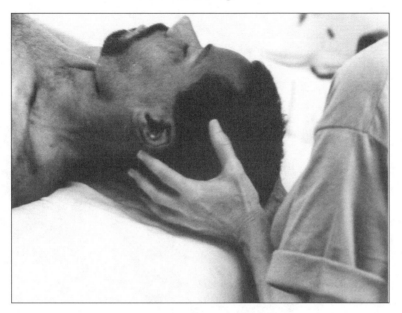

14 Return the head to the center and hold it quietly for a few seconds. Notice how the receiver is breathing; notice the face; notice how this position allows you to see them as a mother might see a sleeping child. Breathe. Slowly remove your hands.

Bowing

Peace to you
Peace to all!

Preparations for Massaging the Neck and Shoulders from a Chair Position

Position

This massage can be given to a person sitting in a wheel chair, in a straight back chair, at a kitchen table, at a desk in an office, or in a teacher's lounge; in other words, almost anywhere. If it is appropriate, you might suggest that your partner remove his or her

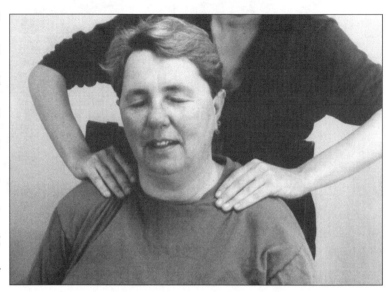

shoes to relax the feet. Place a small pillow beneath the feet and another one behind the back. Remove necklaces, chains, glasses or earrings, particularly long earrings.

Equipment and Environment

◆ appropriate chair

◆ several small pillows

◆ since the person will be fully clothed neither oil nor lotion will be necessary

◆ tape recorder and soothing music, if desired

◆ a special symbol that evokes a sense of reverence and peace, such as a candle, flower, picture of a peaceful scene or holy person

Try to make the massage environment as quiet and peaceful as you can. Be attentive to blocking out as many distractions as possible: take the phone off the hook, put a little sign on the door, or go to a certain part of a space that's away from the flow of people and business.

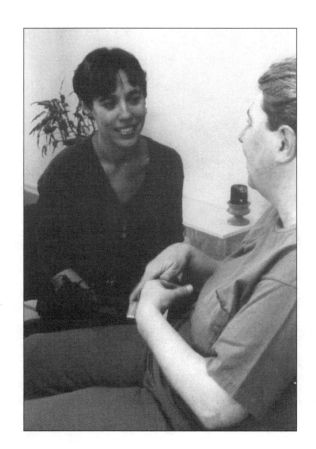

Assessment

Take a couple of minutes before you begin the massage to inquire about how the person is feeling. Remember to ask about any previous injuries in the areas of the neck and shoulders, such as sports injuries or whip lashes. Caring through touch begins in the attentive and receptive way we listen not only with our hands, but with our ears and our hearts, to what the other person has to tell us.

Shoulder Massage

I give you a new commandment: love one another;
just as I have loved you.
– Jesus

Centering

1 Stand behind the person. Take a moment to dedicate this time to easing some of the burdens this person may be carrying. Then let your hands come to rest gently on the shoulders. You will communicate your caring presence through this laying on of hands.

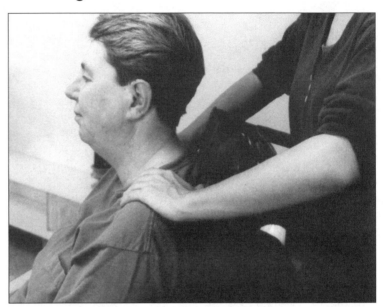

Sweeping

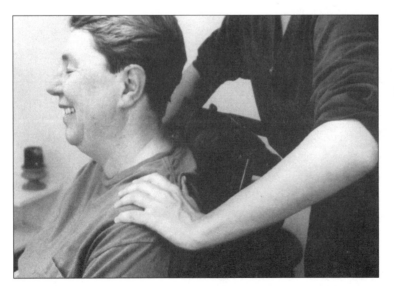

2 Lean weight into your hands and slowly stroke out across the shoulders.

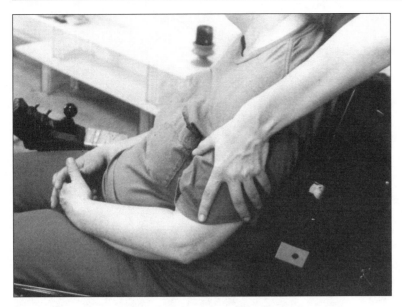

3 Sweep your hands down a little ways into the upper arms; then slide them back up to the shoulders.

Squeezing

4 Drape your hands over the tops of the shoulders. Gather up the muscles here and squeeze them between your palms and fingers. Work from either side of the neck out to the edges of the shoulders and back again. Be careful not to squeeze

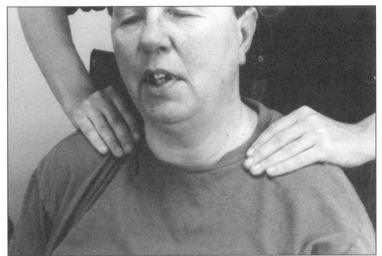

or press down on the collar bones in front of the neck (clavicle). Notice how the muscles feel here and let your fingers and heart respond skillfully and compassionately.

Kneading across the Trapezius

5 Rest your hands on the shoulders with your thumbs resting side by side in the middle of the upper back. Lean the weight of your body into your hands while moving your thumbs in slow rhythmical circles all across the muscles of the upper back, beginning in the center on either side of the spine

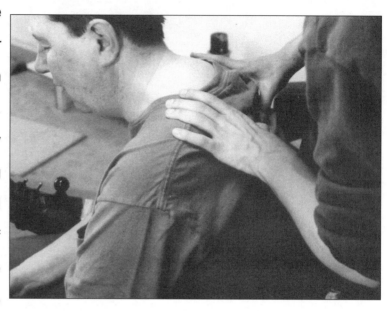

and working out across the shoulders. Concentrate on moving the muscle beneath the clothing and not just the clothing itself. Move back and forth along the upper trapezius several times.

Kneading between the Shoulder Blades

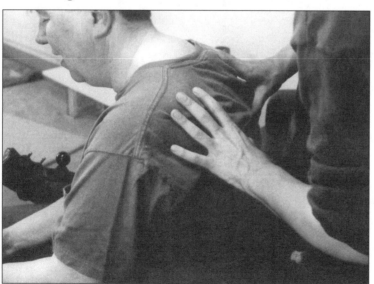

6 Now use your thumbs to do slow circular movements along the inner edges of the shoulder blades (scapula) and the spaces between the shoulder blades and the spine (the rhomboids). Work slowly and firmly here, but gently as this can be a very sensitive and

guarded area for some people. As you work, remember to keep your knees soft and to remain well grounded through your feet.

Circling the Rhomboids and the Scapula (from the opposite side)

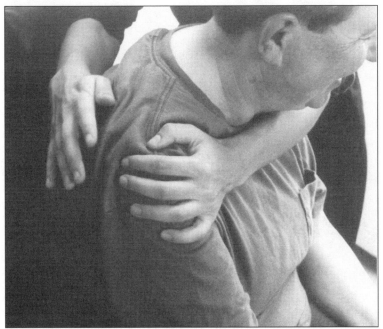

7 Stand at the person's side; rest your arm across the front of the upper chest just below the clavicle. Wrap your fingers around the edge of the shoulder for support. With the palm of your other hand do slow firm palm circles over the shoulder blade.

Holding

8 Gently slide both hands to the center of the upper back and the chest (the heart space). Hold the person here for a few moments. Let love and care flow from your hands.

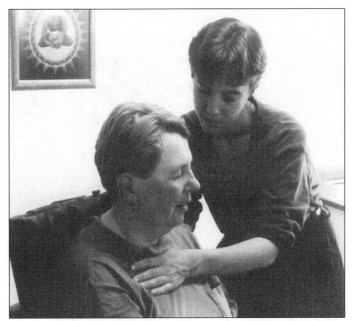

Brushing the Arm

9 Position the palms of your hands at the top of the shoulder. Brush slowly and firmly down the arm and off at the fingertips. Let your soothing hands encourage the muscles to let go of all clinging.

There where our clinging
to things ends, is where
God begins to be.
– Meister Eckhart

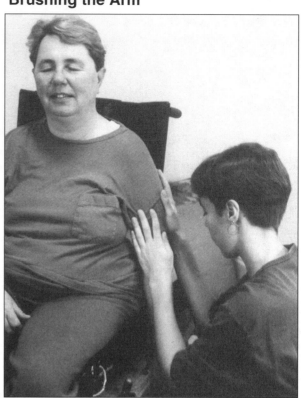

Squeezing/Releasing

10 Wrap both hands around the upper arm and begin an easy rhythmic pattern of squeezing/releasing as you move from the shoulder down to the hands. Work in tandem with your breathing – squeezing: inhaling and filling; releasing: exhaling and emptying.

11 When you come to the hand, sandwich it between your own hands and brush slowly off over the fingertips.

12 Step around to the other side of the person and repeat numbers 8-12.

Resting

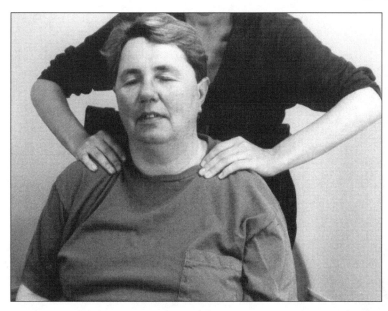

13 Step back behind your partner; place your hands on the shoulders and recognize "the person that each one is in God's eyes." Thomas Merton says, "If only we could see each other that way all the time there would be no more war, no more hatred, no more cruelty, no more greed.... I suppose ...we would all fall down and worship each other."

Neck Massage

Positioning

14 Stand at the person's side. rest one hand over the back of the head and the other over the brow.

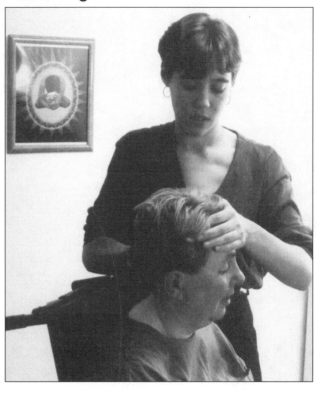

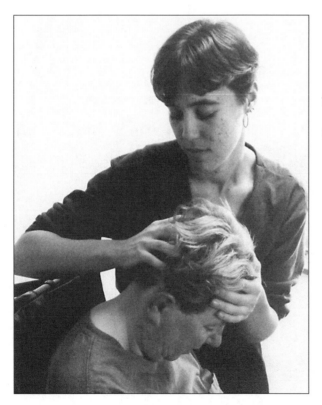

15 Gently bend the head forward to rest in your hand. Be careful that your front hand does not accidentally slip down over the eyes.

Neck Kneading

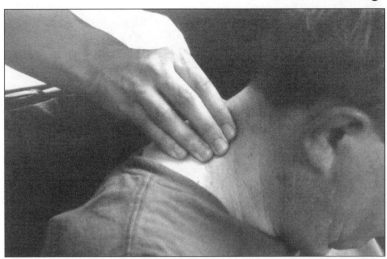

16 Stroke your hand up and down the length of the neck, squeezing and kneading these muscles gently but firmly between your fingers and your thumb. Work slowly and carefully. The neck is a strong and often congested bridge between the head and the rest of the body. Massage here can help to open up the flow of traffic between one's thoughts and feelings.

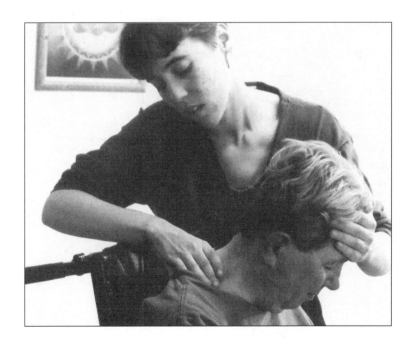

Circling under the Occipital Ridge

17 With your thumb and fingertips carefully circle across the muscles that run along the occipital ridge itself (a bony shelf along the base of the skull). Nerves and tendons from the head, neck and face reside here, often making this area quite tender. These small slow circling movements can help release tension and increase circulation to the head.

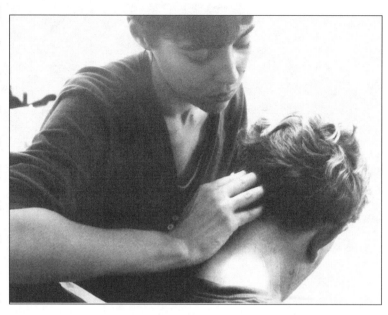

Finishing Touch

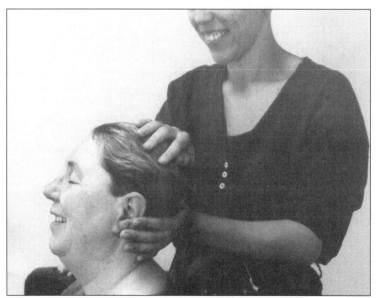

18 Step behind your partner; sweep the front hand over the forehead back through the hair and down the back of the head.

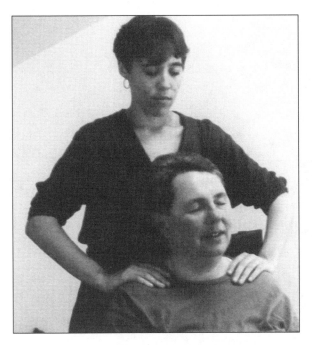

19 Rest your hands peacefully on the tops of the shoulders. You know these shoulders now, and they know your hands. Sacred touch is a very powerful way to embody the "new commandment, love one another as I have loved you" (John 13:34) and to communicate how much you care about another person. It is so simple, so natural and so healing. When it feels right, quietly let your hands slip away.

Bowing

Peace to you
Peace to all!

Head and Face

You anoint my head with oil, my cup overflows.
Surely goodness and mercy shall follow me
all the days of my life.
— Psalm 23

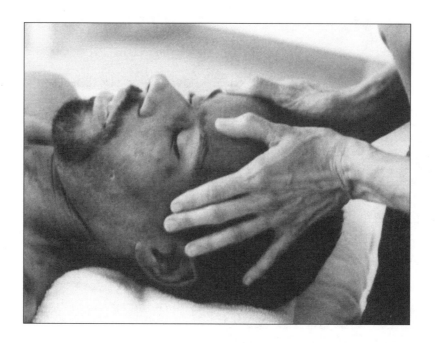

*T*he face with its capacity for expression, is one of the most revealing parts of the human body. Our expressions can create a mask behind which we hide from others and even ourselves, or they can be the open revelation of the true self, in which nothing is hidden, and joy and wisdom are radiated. It is the eyes, "the windows of the soul," that reveal the health of the body: are they full of life, or hollow and vacant? Are they near-sighted (more reclusive, focused on fine detail) or far-sighted (less in touch with immediate reality, more visionary)? The mouth too communicates much by the way it moves and by the words it speaks. The nose that inhales the breath of life, the ears that hear the sounds of creation, the invisible "third eye" in the forehead's center are areas to be touched reverently in massage.

Benefits of Head and Face Massage

A caring and skilled head and face massage can benefit a person in the following ways:

◆ Head: relieves tension and sinus-related headaches by loosening the scalp and relaxing the muscles at the base of the skull, around the temples and over the forehead. Increases circulation to the scalp and to the blood vessels that nourish the hair follicles.

◆ Eyes: relieves tension, strain and fatigue caused by sensitivity to light, natural or artificial, and from using the eyes excessively. The slow precise circling of the eyes and temples may also help to surface withheld feelings in a healthy and healing way.

◆ Sinuses: relieves nasal congestion created by swollen membranes inside the sinus cavities that surround the nose and eyes.

◆ Jaw and TMJ (temporomandibular joint)): Releases tension and spasms in the jaw due to grinding the teeth and clenching the jaw.

◆ Skin: improves circulation, thereby making one's complexion more vibrant and radiant.

◆ Relieves neck tension, reduces mental stress and improves the functioning of the mind. Softens the muscles that communicate outwardly what one is feeling inwardly.

◆ Restores a sense of beauty and self-worth.

◆ Gives one a profound experience of tenderness and well-being.

Conditions, Precautions and Contraindications
for Head and Face Massage

◆ **General**: The face is often quite oily. Use only a small amount of oil/lotion.

◆ **Hair:** Be sensitive to keeping oil or lotion away from the hair as much as possible. Inquire if the person minds having the head and hair touched.

◆ **Contact Lenses**: Inquire as to whether a person is wearing contacts. If so, do not massage over the eyes unless the person removes the lenses.

◆ **Hearing Aids**: Hearing aids are very sensitive. When working around the head or face you may want to suggest that the person remove the devices for this part of the massage.

◆ **Acne**: Ask the person if there is any area of the face where he/she does not wish to be touched.

◆ **Cold Sores** (herpes simplex): Do not apply pressure over the cheeks, lips or mouth area. Do not touch cold sores or massage near them if they are open and draining, or you may spread the infection to the eye.

◆ **Head Colds**: For symptoms such as runny nose and watery eyes, sneezing and coughing, elevate the head to avoid nasal congestion. Always be sure to wash your hands thoroughly before and after the massage.

◆ **Lice**: Do not massage the scalp if there is evidence of lice.

The Physical Anatomy of the Head and Face

Bones

The head and face are held together by twenty-three bones that fit together like an intricate jigsaw puzzle. The cranium (skull) is made up of four bones: the frontal (forehead and front portion of skull), temporals (temples), occipital (back of skull), and the parietal (sides of the skull running between the frontal and occipital bones.)

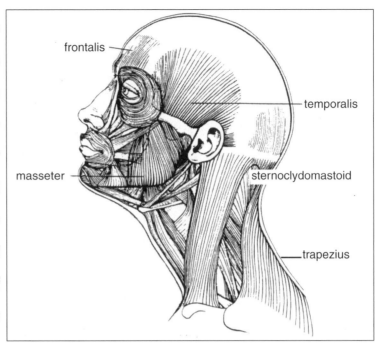

Some of the finely chiseled bones in the face are the orbits (eye sockets), the nasal bone, the mandible (jaw), the maxilla (upper jaw bone), and the zygomatic bones (cheeks).

Muscles

The intricate layers of muscles of the face give each person a unique look and help to create an endless number of expressions to either mask or reveal true feelings.

The following are a few of the more superficial muscles:

A very thin layer of muscle tissue covers the skull. Scalp massage will help relieve the build-up of pressure here that tightens the skin and contributes to headaches and eye strain. The frontalis is a thin muscle over the forehead that moves the eyebrows up and down and wrinkles the brow with "worry lines." The muscles that function in the opening and closing of the jaws are the masseters and the temporalis. You can feel the masseter muscle by placing your fingers over the jaw joint and clenching your teeth. Place your fingers just below your cheek bones (zygomatic arch) and clench your teeth, and you will feel the temporalis muscle.

Tension in these two muscles can easily lead to headaches or jaw misalignment. Don't skip massaging them!

Besides these superficial muscles, there are a multitude of others in the face used for self-expression. All of these muscles will be stimulated when you follow the contours of the face throughout the massage.

The muscles of the head and face are directly influenced by the muscles in the neck and shoulder, particularly the trapezius muscle which connects to the occipital bone, and the sternoclyidomastoid muscles which connect to the mastoid process and make it possible for the head to turn from side to side. For this reason it is a good idea to massage the neck and shoulders before doing the head and face.

Preparations for Massaging the Head and Face

Position

Have the person lie down on a comfortable but firm surface. A massage table is ideal. Otherwise place a thick piece of foam on the floor and cover it with a flannel sheet. Place a pillow beneath the knees to provide extra support to the low back and

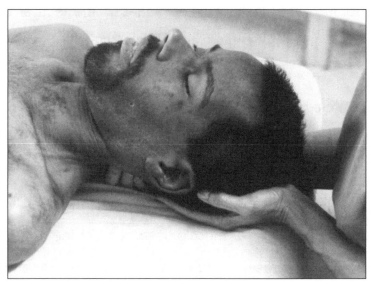

ease the pelvis. If the person is wearing a blouse or shirt you may suggest that it be removed in order to do a little massage around the neck and shoulders. In this case you would always cover the person with a sheet. Otherwise, work over the clothes without staining them with the oil/lotion. As the giver, stand or sit behind the head. If you stand, be sensitive not to overpower the person with your presence. If you sit, be careful that you don't withdraw too much. There is a very fine balance in presence to be achieved here as you work in one of the most intimate parts of the body.

Equipment and Environment

◆ oil or lotion. If you are including the face in a full massage, you may continue to use oil, but sparingly since the face secretes its own oil. If you are going to be giving just a face massage, lotion is usually the best choice. Never use a scented lotion/oil without first inquiring if the person has any allergic reactions to scents.

◆ candle, fresh flowers, quiet music if appropriate

◆ extra pillows, towels and blankets for warmth and comfort

Assessment

Ask the person if there is anything that you should know or they would like to tell you about this area of their body before beginning the massage. Some general areas of concern may have to do with the hair, eyes and skin conditions. If a person is going to go on to other appointments after the massage, you will want to assure them that you will not be getting oil/lotion in the hair, nor will you be disturbing the hair style. Inquire about contact lenses. If the person is not going to be removing them, you will not want to work directly over the eyes. Ask about any skin conditions that might be of concern regarding pressure or lotion. Inquire about areas of the face where the person may be noticing tension, such as corners of the mouth, jaw, eyes, forehead. Listen carefully so you will be able to bring additional attention to these places.

The Massage Sequence

May we see Christ's loving face;
may we be an icon of his grace.
– chant

Centering and Laying on of Hands

1 Lay your hands quietly against the sides of the person's head and face. Breathe, take the opportunity to really look at this face and to listen to it through your hands, your eyes and your heart. This is the face of Christ, today.

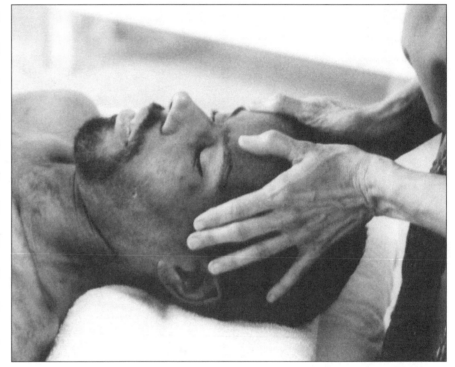

Cradling the Head

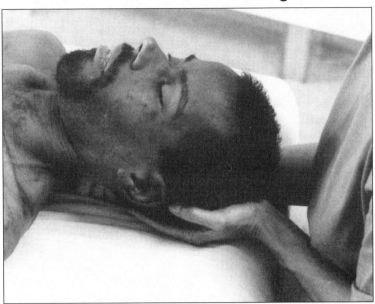

2 Slip your hands beneath the head and neck. Cradle the head for a moment. Imagine the warmth of your hands penetrating the cranium and bathing the mind with peace.

Kneading the Scalp

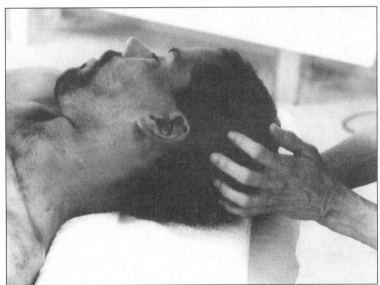

3 Turn the head to one side; let it rest in the palm of your hand while you use the fingertips of your other hand to knead the thin layer of muscle that covers the skull (cranium). Really concentrate on moving the scalp and not just the hair. Turn the head from one side to the other while working here so you can cover the entire head.

4 Give some extra attention to the muscles at the base of the skull. When these muscles are tight, as they often are, they can be the cause of many headaches.

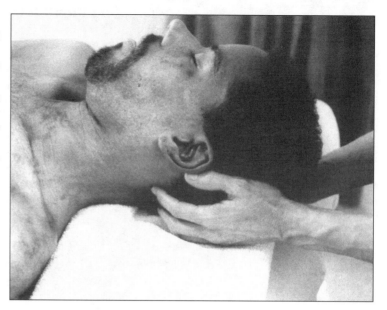

Resting on the Forehead

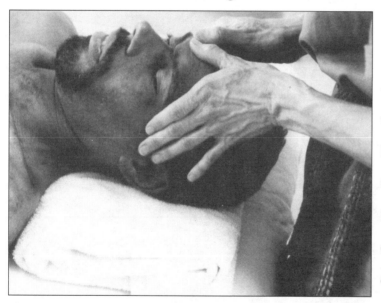

5 Position your hands on either side of the head and rest your thumbs in the middle of the forehead just above the eyebrows. In many sacred traditions this point between the eyes is believed to be the center of wisdom; it has been called the "third eye" and "God's eye," referring to a reality that is beyond discrimination and segregation. Gently holding this point may awaken feelings of wholeness and beauty and bring a sense of calm to a troubled mind. This is the "art" of presence.

Stroking the Forehead

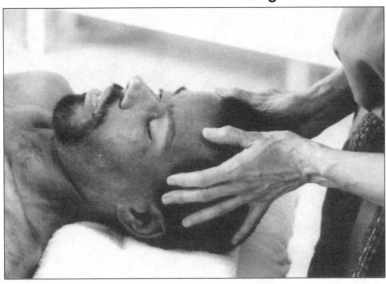

6 Pull your thumbs over the brow, out to the sides of the head and off. Let your stroking be firm and full, never quick or harsh. Stroke in this pattern, moving from above the eyebrows back to the hairline. Be aware that the brain rests just behind this frontal bone, so any sensations that are felt here will be transmitted directly to the brain and from there to the rest of the body. Let your movements create sensations of peace and trust, and genuine care.

Stroking above the Eye

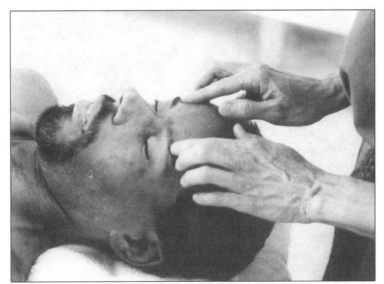

7 Rest your fingers in the center of the brow between the eyebrows and stroke out over the eye brows; let your fingers feel the upper rim of the bony eye sockets.

Circling the Temples

8 Sink your fingers into the temples and circle this area slowly and mindfully. Applied pressure here can calm both the eyes and the mind.

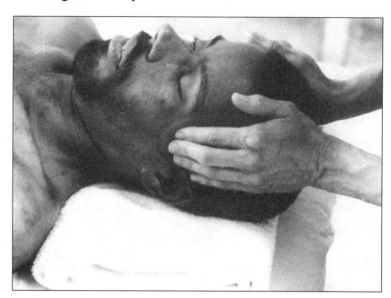

Stroking beneath the Eye

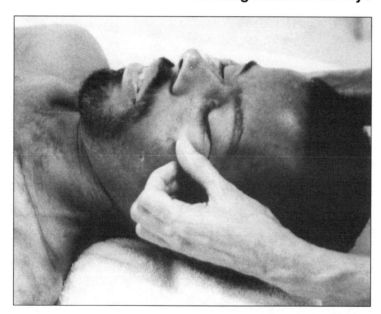

9 Rest your thumbs against the inner corners of the eyes and stroke across the lower bony eye rim and back to the temples. There may be some very tender places here due to eye strain and the proximity of sinus cavities. Circle the temples again.

Stroking over the Eyes

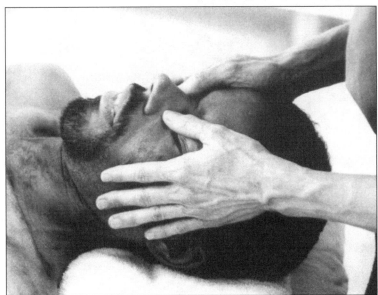

10 Cup your hands around the face, resting your thumbs like small pillows over the eyes. Slowly and steadily stroke out over the eyes.

Stroking/Circling the Cheek Bones

11 Stroke your thumbs over the cheek bones; then do small thumb circles, moving from the sides of the nose to the sides of the face.

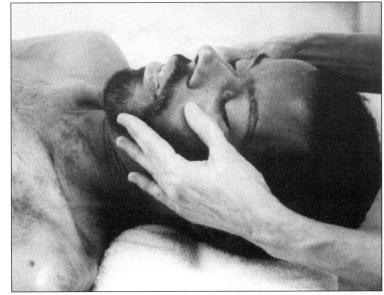

Kneading the Nose

12 Use your index and third fingers to do small slow, circular movements down along the side of the nose.

Stroking the Upper Lip

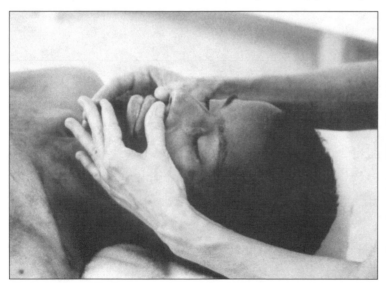

13 Rest your fingers beneath the chin and place your thumbs side by side in the middle of the upper lip beneath the nose. Receive the breath here. Stroke out to the corners of the mouth. Circle the corners with your fingertips.

Stroking below the Lip

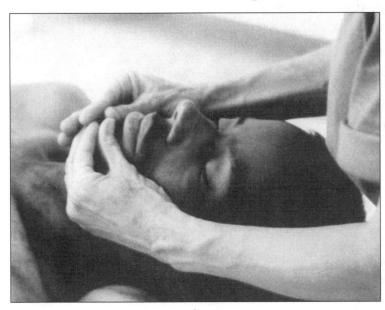

14 Cup the chin between your thumbs and fingers. Pull the thumbs out across the chin.

Circling the TM Joint

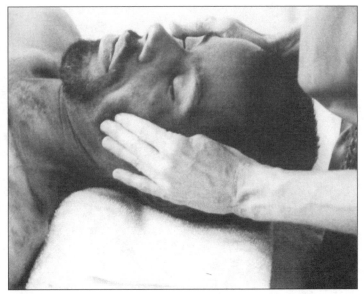

15 Stroke up the jaw to where the jaw (mandible) and the temporalis bones meet, otherwise known as the TM joint. Lean your fingers into the spaces between these two bones. Do slow, firm finger circles. This is one of the most troublesome joints in the body – a place where we clench our teeth, hold back our words, our tears, our sighs and our praise.

Stroking the Ears

16 Grasp the ear lobes between your fingers and gently pull them downwards; slide up to the middle of the ears and gently stretch them out to the sides; slip up to the tops of the ears and pull them upwards. Breathe; hear this person's life through your fingertips.

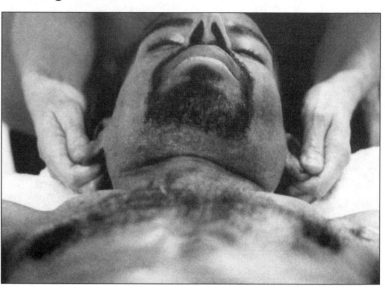

Stroking the Jaw

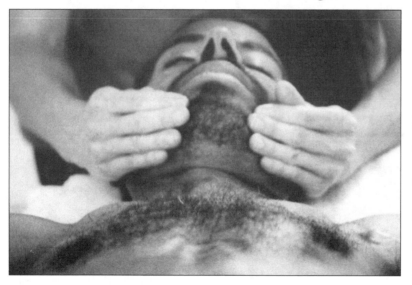

17 Cup your hands beneath the chin. Slowly and tenderly draw your hands up the sides of the face to the temples and off. Repeat this comforting stroke several times. Be like a sculptor stroking and beholding.

Rest

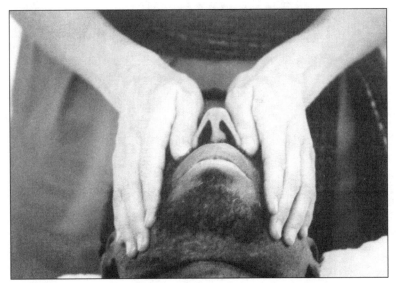

18 Softly rest your hands, like warm blankets of love, over the face. Breathe. Slowly let your hands open as a flower opens to the sun.

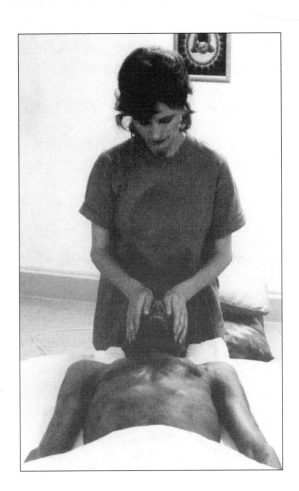

Bowing

*Peace to you
Peace to all!*

Bibliography

Ministry

Cassidy, Sheila. *A Good Friday People*. Maryknoll, N.Y.: Orbis Books, 1991.

————. *Sharing the Darkness: The Spirituality of Caring*. Maryknoll, N.Y.: Orbis Books, 1991.

Dass, Ram, and Mirabai Bush. *Compassion in Action*. New York: Bell Tower, 1992.

Dass, Ram, and Paul Gorman. *How Can I Help?* New York: Alfred A. Knopf, 1985.

Eppsteiner, Fred. *The Path of Compassion: Writings on Socially Engaged Buddhism*. Berkeley, Calif.: Parallax Press, 1988.

Fox, Matthew. *A Spirituality Named Compassion and the Healing of the Global Village, Humpty Dumpty and Us*. Minneapolis: Winston Press, 1979.

Frankl, Victor. *Man's Search for Meaning*. New York: Washington Square Press, 1985.

Gateley, Edwina. *I Hear a Seed Growing: God of the Streets*. Trabuco Canyon, Calif.: Source Books, 1990.

Kelsey, Morton T. *Caring: How Can We Love One Another?*. New York: Paulist Press, 1981.

Levine, Stephen. *A Gradual Awakening*. New York: Anchor Press/Doubleday, 1979.

Luks, Allan, and Peggy Payne. *The Healing Power of Doing Good: The Health and Spiritual Benefits of Helping Others*. New York: Balantine Books, 1991.

Nouwen, Henri, J. M. *The Wounded Healer*. New York: Image Books, 1979.

————. *The Way of the Heart*. San Francisco, Calif.: Harper and Row, 1981.

————. *Reaching Out: The Three Movements of the Spiritual Life*. New York: Image Books, 1986.

Serrou, Robert. *Teresa of Calcutta*. New York: McGraw-Hill, 1980.

Spink, Kathryn, and Jean and Larche Vanier. *A Communion of Love*. New York: Crossroad, 1991.

Teresa, Mother. *One Heart Full of Love*. Grand Rapids, Michigan: Servant Books, 1991.

Vanier, Jean. *The Broken Body: A Journey to Wholeness*. New York: Paulist Press,1988.

Poetry and Scripture

Cousineau, Phil, and Eric Lawton. *The Soul of the World: A Modern Book of Hours*. San Francisco: Harper San Francisco, 1993.

Harvey, Andrew.*The Way of Passion: A Celebration of Rumi.* Berkeley: Frog,1991.

Mitchell, Stephen. *The Enlightened Heart: An Anthology of Sacred Poetry.* New York: Harper and Row, 1989.

Rilke, Rainer Maria. *New Poems 1908: The Other Part.* San Francisco: North Point Press, 1987.

Roberts, Elizabeth A., and Elias Amidon. *Earth Prayers*. San Francisco: Harper San Francisco, 1991.

Satchidananda, Sri Swami. *The Living Gita: The Complete Bhagavad Gita and Commentary*. New York: Henry Holt, 1988.

Star, Johnathan. *Two Suns Rising: A Collection of Sacred Writings.* New York: Bantam Books, 1991.

The Bhagavad Gita. London: Penguin Books, 1962.

The New English Bible with the Apocrapha. New York: Oxford University Press, 1976.

Ministry with the Dying

Feinstein, David, and Peg Elliot Mayo. *Rituals for Living and Dying.* San Francisco: Harper San Francisco, 1990.

Kubler-Ross, Elisabeth. *To Live Until We Say Good-Bye*. New York: Simon and Schuster, 1978.

Levine, Stephen. *Who Dies? An Investigation of Conscious Living and Conscious Dying.* New York: Anchor Press/Doubleday, 1982.

Nuland, Sherwin *B. How We Die: Reflections on Life's Final Chapter.* New York: Alfred A. Knopf, 1994.

Rinpoche, Sogyal. *The Tibetan Book of Living and Dying.* San Francisco: Harper San Francisco, 1992.

Rupp, Joyce, OSM. *Praying Our Goodbyes.* Notre Dame, Ind.: Ave Maria Press, 1988.

Maternity

Klaus, Dr. Marshall H., and Dr. John H. Kennell. *Mothering the Mother: How a Doula Can Help You Have A Shorter, Easier, And Healtheir Birth.* New York: Addison-Wesley Publishing, 1993.

McClure, Vimala. *The Tao of Motherhood.* Willow Springs, Mo.: Nucleus Pub., 1991.

Ministry of Care

Barstow, Cedar, M.Ed. *Tending Body and Spirit: Massage and Counseling with Elders.* Boulder, Colo.: Boulder Press, 1985.

Bell, Lorna, R.N., and Eudora Seyfer. *Gentle Yoga: Yoga for People with Arthritis, Stroke Damage, Multiple Sclerosis, in Wheelchairs, or Anyone Who Needs a Guide to Gentle Exercise.* Berkeley, Calif.: Celestial Arts, 1987.

Clarke, Rita-Lou. *Pastoral Care of Battered Women.* Philadelphia: Westminister Press, 1986.

Doress, Paula Brown, and Diana Laskin Siegal. *Ourselves, Growing Older.* New York: Simon and Schuster, 1987.

Godfrey, Dr. Charles and, Michael Feldman. *The Ageless Exercise Plan: A Complete Guide to Fitness after Fifty.* New York: McGraw-Hill, 1984.

Greenberg, Carol, with Stein, Sara. *Pretend Your Nose Is a Crayon.* Boston: Houghton Mifflin, 1991.

Karr, Katherine L. *Taking Time for Me: How Caregivers Can Effectively Deal with Stress.* Buffalo, N.Y.: Prometheus Books,1992.

Kent, Howard. *Yoga for the Disabled.* New York: Thorsons Publishing Group, 1985.

Luce, Gay Gaer. *Longer Life, More Joy: Techniques for Enhancing Health, Happiness and Inner Vision.* North Hollywood, Calif.: Newcastle Publishing, 1992.

Muller, Wayne. *Legacy of the Heart: The Spiritual Advantages of a Painful Childhood.* New York: Simon and Schuster, 1992.

Noble, Elizabeth. *Essential Exercises for the Childbearing Years.* Boston: Houghton Mifflin, 1988.

Nouwen, Henri, J.M., and Walter J. Gaffney. *Aging: The Fulfillment of Life*. New York: Doubleday, 1974.

O'Connor, Elizabeth. *Cry Pain, Cry Hope: Thresholds to Purpose*. Waco, Tex.: Word Books, 1987.

Ohashi, Wataru, with Mary Hoover. *Natural Childbirth, The Eastern Way: A Healthy Pregnancy and Delivery Through Shiatsu*. New York: Ballantine Books, 1983.

Stillerman, Elaine. *Mother Massage*. New York: Dell Publishing, 1992.

Tate, David A. *Health Hope and Healing*. New York: M. Evans, 1989.

Travis, John W., M.D.,and Meryn G. Callander. *Wellness for Helping Professionals: Creating Compassionate Cultures*. Mill Valley, Calif.: Wellness Associates Publications, 1990.

Theology

Borg, Marcus J. *Meeting Jesus Again for the First Time: The Historical Jesus and the Heart of Contemporary Faith*. San Francisco, Calif.: Harper San Francisco, 1994.

Brown, Norman O. *Love's Body*. New York: Vintage Books, 1966.

Davis, Charles. *Body as Spirit: The Nature of Religious Feeling*. New York: Seabury Press, 1976.

Eck, Diana L. *Encountering God: A Spiritual Journey from Bozeman to Banaras*. Boston: Beacon Press, 1993.

Empereur, James L., S.J. *Prophetic Anointing: God's Call to the Sick, the Elderly, and the Dying*. Wilmington, Delaware: Michael Glazier, 1982.

Fenton, John Y. (Ed). *Theology and Body*. Philadelphia: Westminster Press, 1974.

Fox, Matthew. *Original Blessing*. Santa Fe, N. M.: Bear and Co., 1983.

Keating, Thomas. *Open Mind, Open Heart: The Contemplative Dimension of the Gospel*. Rockport, Mass.: Element, 1992.

McBride, Denis, C.Ss.R. *Impressions of Jesus* . Quezon City, Philippines: Claretian Publications, 1993.

Miles, Margaret R. *Carnal Knowing: Female Nakedness and Religious Meaning in the Christian West.* Boston, Mass.: Beacon Press, 1989.

Mitchell, Stephen. *The Gospel According to Jesus.* New York: Harper Collins, 1991.

Mollenkott, Virginia Ramey. *Sensuous Spirituality: Out from Fundamentalism.* New York: Crossroad, 1992.

Nelson, James B. *Between Two Gardens: Reflections on Sexuality and Religious Experience.* New York: Pilgrim Press, 1983.

Nouwen, Henri, J.M. *The Return of the Prodigal Son: A Meditation on Fathers, Brothers, and Sons.* New York: Doubleday, 1992.

Tillich, Paul. *The Meaning of Health: The Relation of Religion and Health.* Richmond, Calif.: North Atlantic Books, 1981.

Von Durckheim, Karlfried Graf. *Hara: The Vital Centre of Man.* Boston: Mandala Books, 1977.

Walker, James Lynwood. *Body and Soul: Gestalt Therapy and Religious Experience.* Nashville: Abingdon Press, 1971.

Spiritual Life and Practices

Beck, Charlotte Joko. *Everyday Zen: Love and Work.* San Francisco, Calif.: Harper and Row, 1989.

Campbell, Peter A., Ph.D., and Edwin M. McMahon, Ph.D. *Bio-Spirituality: Focusing as a Way to Grow.* Chicago: Loyola University Press, 1985.

Dass, Ram. *Journey of Awakening: A Meditator's Guidebook.* New York: Bantam Books, 1978.

Dorff, Francis. *The Art of Passingover: An Invitation to Living Creatively.* New York: Paulist Press, 1988.

Egan, Eileen, and Kathleen Egan, O.S.B. *Blessed Are You: Mother Teresa and the Beatitudes.* Ann Arbor, Mich.: Servant Publications, 1992.

Fields, Taylor, Weyler, and Ingrasci. *Chop Wood Carry Water: A Guide to Finding Spiritual Fulfillment in Everyday Life.* Los Angeles, Calif.: Jeremy P. Tarcher, 1984.

Finley, James. *The Awakening Call: Fostering Intimacy with God.* Notre Dame, Ind.: Ave Maria Press, 1984.

Fox, Matthew. *The Reinvention of Work: A New Vision of Livelihood for Our Time.* San Francisco, Calif.: Harper San Francisco, 1994.

Grigg, Ray, *The Tao of Being.* Atlanta: Humanics New Age, 1989.

Hanh, Thich Nhat. *Being Peace.* Berkeley, Calif.: Parallax Press, 1987.

—————. *The Blooming of a Lotus.* Boston: Beacon Press, 1993.

—————. *The Miracle of Mindfulness.* Boston: Beacon Press, 1975.

—————. *Peace Is Every Step.* New York: Bantam Books, 1991.

—————. *Present Moment Wonderful Moment.* Berkeley, Calif.: Parallax Press, 1990.

—————. *Touching Peace.* Berkeley, Calif.: Parallax Press, 1992.

Harris, Maria. *Dance of the Spirit: The Seven Steps of Women's Spirituality.* New York: Bantam Books, 1989.

Housden, Roger. *Fire In the Heart: Everyday Life as Spiritual Practice.* London: Element Books, 1990.

Huges, Louis. *Body Mind and Spirit: To Harmony through Meditation.* Mystic, Conn.: Twenty-Third Publications, 1990.

Johnston, William. *Being In Love: The Practice of Christian Prayer.* San Francisco, Calif.: Harper and Row, Publishers, 1989.

Kabat-Zinn, Jon. *Wherever You Go There You Are: Mindfulness Meditation in Everyday Life.* New York: Hyperion, 1994.

Kaufer, Nelly, and Carol Osmer-Newhouse. *A Woman's Guide to Spiritual Renewal.* San Francisco, Calif.: Harper San Francisco, 1994.

Louden, Jennifer. *The Woman's Comfort Book: A Self-Nurturing Guide for Restoring Balance in Your Life.* San Francisco, Calif.: Harper San Francisco, 1992.

Miller, Ronald S. *As Above So Below: Paths to Spiritual Renewal in Daily Life.* Los Angeles: Jeremy P. Tarcher, 1992.

Moore, Thomas. *Care of the Soul: A Guide for Cultivating Depth and Sacredness in Everyday Life.* New York: Harper Collins, 1992.

Mueller Nelson, Gertrud. *To Dance with God: Family Ritual and Community Celebration.* New York: Paulist Press, 1986.

Nouwen, Henri, J.M. *With Open Hands: Bring Prayer into Your Life.* New York: Ballantine Books, 1972.

—————. *Out of Solitude: Three Meditations on the Christian Life.* Notre Dame, Ind.: Ave Maria Press, 1974.

Richards, M.C. *Centering: In Pottery, Poetry, and the Person.* Middletown, Conn.: Wesleyan University Press, 1989.

O'Brien, Justin. *Christianity and Yoga: A Meeting of Mystic Paths.* New York: Viking Penguin, 1989.

Rupp, Joyce. *May I Have This Dance?* Notre Dame, Ind.: Ave Maria Press, 1992.

Sheldrake, Philip, S.J. *Images of Holiness: Explorations in Contemporary Spirituality.* Notre Dame, Ind.: Ave Maria Press, 1988.

Steindl-Rast, Brother David. *Gratefulness, the Heart of Prayer: An Approach to Life in Fullness.* Ramsey, NJ: Paulist Press, 1984.

Penguin Classics. *The Upanishads.* London: Penguin Books, 1965.

Walker, Susan. *Speaking of Silence: Christians and Buddhists on the Contemplative Way.* New York: Paulist Press, 1987.

Welwood, John. *Ordinary Magic: Everyday Life as Spiritual Path.* Boston, Mass: Shambhala, 1992.

Anatomy

Bruun, Ruth Dowling, M.D., and Bertel Bruun, M.D. *The Human Body: Your Body and How it Works.* New York: Random House, 1982.

Donnelly, Joseph E. *Living Anatomy.* Second Edition. Champaign, Ill.: Human Kinetics Books, 1990.

Jolly, Dr. Richard T. *The Color Atlas of Human Anatomy.* New York: Harmony Books, 1980.

Miller, Johathan. *The Human Body, with Three-Dimensional, Movable Illustrations Showing the Workings of the Human Body.* New York: Viking, 1983.

Olsen, Andrea. *Body Stories: A Guide to Experiential Anatomy.* New York: Station Hill Press, 1991.

Potamkin, Gail and Decaro, Matthew V. *The Gray's Anatomy Coloring Book.* Philadelphia, 1980.

Sieg, Kay W., Ph.D., and Sandra P. Adams, ., Ph.D. *Illustrated Essentials of Musculoskeletal Anatomy.* Second Edition. Gainesville, Fla.: Mega Books, 1985.

Energy

Brennan, Barbara Ann. *Hands of Light: A Guide to Healing Through the Human Energy Field.* New York: Bantam Books, 1987.

Gunther, Bernard. *Energy, Ecstasy and Your Seven Vital Chakras.* North Hollywood, Calif.: Newcastle, 1983

Judith, Anodea. *Wheels of Life: A User's Guide to the Chakra System.* St. Paul, Minn.: Llewellyn Publications, 1987.

Mann, John, and Lar Short. *The Body of Light: History and Practical Techniques for Awakening Your Subtle Body.* New York: Globe Press, 1990.

Schwarz, Jack. *Voluntary Controls: Exercises for Creative Meditation and for Activating the Potential of the Chakras.* New York: E.P. Dutton, 1978.

Body Awareness Reading

Brooks, Charles V. W. *Sensory Awareness: The Rediscovery of Experiencing.* New York: Viking Press, 1974.

Conger, John P. *Jung and Reich: The Body as Shadow.* Berkeley, Calif.: North Atlantic Books, 1988.

Dychtwald, Ken. *Bodymind: A Synthesis of Eastern and Western Ways to Self-Awareness, Health, and Personal Growth.* New York: Pantheon Books, 1977.

Foster, Patricia. *Minding the Body: Women Writers on Body and Soul.* New York: Doubleday, 1994.

Heckler, Richard Strozzi. *The Anatomy of Change: East/West Approaches to Body/Mind Therapy.* Boulder, Colo.: Shambhala, 1984.

Heller, Joseph, and William Henkin. *Bodywise: Regaining Your Natural Flexibility and Vitality for Maximum Well-Being.* Los Angeles, Calif.: Jeremy P. Tarcher, 1986.

Hendricks, Gay, Ph.D., and Kathlyn Hendricks, Ph.D. *The Speed of Life: New Approach to Personal Change through Body-Centered Therapy.* New York: Bantam, 1993.

Hutchinson, Marcia Germaine, Ed.D. *Transforming Body Image: Learning to Love the Body You Have.* Freedom, Calif.: Crossing Press, 1985.

Johnson, Don. *Body.* Boston, Mass.: Beacon Press, 1983.

Keleman, Stanley. *Embodying Experience: Forming a Personal Life.* Berkeley, Calif.: Center Press, 1987.

—————. *Somatic Reality: Bodily Experience and Emotional Truth.* Berkeley, Calif.: Center Press, 1979.

—————. *The Human Ground: Sexuality, Self and Survival.* Palo Alto, Calif.: Science and Behavior Books, 1975.

—————. *Your Body Speaks its Mind.* New York: Pocket Books, 1975.

Kirsta, Alix. *The Book of Stress Survival: Identifying and Reducing the Stress in Your Life.* New York: Simon and Schuster, 1986.

Lidell, Lucy. *The Sensual Body: An Ultimate Guide to Body Awareness and Self-Fulfillment.* New York: Simon and Schuster, 1987.

Lilly, John C., M.D. *The Body Reveals: An Illustrated Guide to the Psychology of the Body.* New York: Harper and Row/Quicksilver Books, 1976.

Lowen, Alexander, M.D. *The Spirituality of the Body: Bioenergetics for Grace and Harmony.* New York: Macmillan, 1990.

Ohashi. *Reading the Body: Ohaski's Book of Oriental Diagnosis.* New York: Arkana Books, 1991.

Shapiro, Debbie. *The Bodymind Workbook: Exploring How the Body and the Mind Work Together.* Longmead, Great Britain: Element Books, 1990.

Healer and Healing

Bakken, Kenneth L. *The Call to Wholeness: Health as a Spiritual Journey.* New York: Crossroad, 1985.

Bear, Sun, Crysalis Mulligan, Peter Nufer, and Wabun. *Walk in Balance.* New York: Prentice Hall, 1989.

Braheny, Mary, and Diane Halperin. *Mind, Body, Spirit: Connecting with Your Creative Self.* Deerfield Beach, Fla.: Health Communications, 1989.

Brand, Dr. Paul, and Philip Yancey. *Fearfully and Wonderfully Made: A Surgeon Looks at the Human and Spiritual Body.* Grand Rapids, Mich.: Zondervan Publishing House, 1980.

Brooks, Svevo. *The Art of Good Living: Simple Steps to Regaining Health and the Joy of Life.* Boston, Mass.: Houghton Mifflin, 1990.

Carlson, Richard, Ph.D., and Benjamin Shield. *Healers on Healing.* Los Angeles, Calif.: Jeremy P. Tarcher, 1989.

Chopra, Deepak, M.D. *Ageless Body, Timeless Mind: A Quantum Alternative to Growing Old.* New York: Harmony Books, 1993.

————. *Perfect Health: The Complete Mind/Body Guide.* New York: Harmony Books, 1990.

Bibliography

Cousins, Norman. *Anatomy of an Illness*. New York: Bantam Books, 1980.

Dossey, Larry, M.D. *Beyond Illness: Discovering the Experience of Health*. Boston, Mass.: Shambhala, 1984.

————. *Healing Words: The Power of Prayer and the Practice of Medicine*. San Francisco, Calif.: Harper San Francisco, 1993.

————. *Recovering the Soul: A Scientific and Spiritual Search*. New York: Bantam Books, 1989.

Frank, Arthur W. *At the Will of the Body: Reflections on Illness*. New York: Houghton Mifflin, 1991.

Ingerman, Sandra. *Welcome Home: Life after Healing Following Your Soul's Journey Home*. San Francisco, Calif.: Harper San Francisco, 1993.

Koch, Carl, and Joyce Heil. *Created in God's Image: Meditating on Our Body*. Winona, Minn.: Saint Mary's Press, 1991.

Laskow, Leonard, M.D. *Healing with Love*. San Francisco, Calif.: Harper San Francisco, 1992.

Levine, Stephen. *Healing into Life and Death*. Garden City, N.Y.: Anchor Press/Doubleday, 1987.

Meek, George W. *Healers and the Healing Process*. Wheaton, Ill.: Theosophical Publishing House, 1977.

Miller, Jonathan. *The Body in Question*. New York: Vintage Books, 1982.

Moyers, Bill. *Healing and the Mind*. New York: Doubleday, 1993.

Poole, William. *The Heart of Healing*. Atlanta: Turner Publishing, Inc., 1993.

Sanford, John A. *Healing and Wholeness*. New York: Paulist Press, 1977.

Wuellner, Flora Slosson. *Heart of Healing Heart of Light*. Nashville: Upper Room Books, 1992.

Wuellner, Flora Slosson. *Prayer, Fear, and Our Powers*. Nashville, Tenn.: The Upper Room, 1989

————. *Prayer, Stress, and Our inner Wounds*. Nashville, Tenn.: The Upper Room, 1985.

Touch

Brown, Malcolm, Ph.D. *The Healing Touch: An Introduction to Organismic Psychotherapy*. Mendocino, Calif.: Liferhythm, 1990.

Cohen, Sherry Suib. *The Magic of Touch*. New York: Harper and Row, 1987.

Colton, Helen. *Touch Therapy*. New York: Kensington Publishing, 1989.

Cottingham, John T. *Healing Through Touch: A History and a Review of the Physiological Evidence*. Champaign, Ill.: Broadside Press, 1985.

Davis, Phyllis K. *The Power of Touch*. Carson, Calif.: Hay House, 1991.

Ford, Dr. Clyde W. *Compassionate Touch: The Role of Human Touch in Healing and Recovery*. New York: Fireside/Parkside, 1993.

Gunzenhauser, Brazelton, Field. *Advances in Touch: New Implications in Human Development* Sklllman, N.J.: Johnson and Johnson, (Pediatric Round Table: 14) 1990.

Johnson, Denny. *Touch: Starvation in America: A Call to Arms*. Santa Barbara, Calif.: Rayid Publications, 1985.

Krieger, Dolores, Ph.D., RN. *Accepting Your Power to Heal: The Personal Practice of Therapeutic Touch*. Santa Fe, N.M.: Bear and Company, 1993.

—————. *Living the Therapeutic Touch: Healing as a Lifestyle*. New York: Dodd and Mead, 1987.

McNeely, Anne Deldon. *Touching: Body Therapy and Depth Psychology*. Toronto: Inner City Books, 1987.

Montagu, Asnley. *Touching: The Human Significallce of the Skin*. New York: Harper and Row, 1986.

Older, R. Jules. *Touching Is Healing*. New York: Stein and Day, 1982.

Eastern Style of Massage

Bauer, Cathryn. *Acupressure for Women*. Freedom, Calif.: Crossing Press, 1987.

Gach, Michael Reed. *Acupressure's Potent Points: A Guide to Self-Care for Common Ailments*. New York: Bantam Books, 1990.

Jarmey, Chris, and John Tindall. *Acupressure for Common Ailments*. New York: Simon and Schuster, 1991.

Kuan, Yo-Mo. *Chinese Massage Therapy: A Handbook of Therapeutic Massage*. Boulder, Colo.: Shambhala, 1983.

Lundberg, Paul. *The Book of Shiatsu: A Complete Guide to Using Hand Pressure and Gentle Manipulation to Improve Your Health, Vitality, and Stamina*. New York: Simon and Schuster, 1992.

Rick, Stephanie. *The Reflexology Workout: Hand and Foot Massage for Super Health and Rejuvenation*. New York: Harmony Books, Crown Publishers, 1986.

Sohn, Tina, and Donna Finando. *Amma: The Ancient Art of Oriental Healing*. Rochester, Vt: Healing Arts Press, 1988.

Sokushindo, *The Do-it-Yourself Chinese Foot Massage Therapy*. Japan: Bunka Sosaku Shuppan, 1988.

Teegarden, Iona Marsaa, M.A., M.F.C.C. *The Joy of Feeling: Bodymind Acupressure, Jin Shin Do* . Tokyo and New York: Japan Publications, 1987.

————. *Acupressure Way of Health: Jin Shin Do*. Tokyo and New York: Japan Publications, 1978.

West, Ouida, M.Th. *The Magic of Massage: A New and Holistic Approach*. New York: Putnam, 1983.

General Massage

Harrold, Fiona. *The Complete Body Massage: A Hands-on Manual*. New York: Sterling Publishing, 1992.

Hofer, Jack. *Mini Massage: Ten-to-Fiftenn-Minute Massage Therapies that Reduce Stress*. New York: Putnam, 1988.

Lacroix, Nitya. *Learning Massage in a Weekend*. New York: Alfred A. Knopf, 1992.

————. *Massage for Total Stress Relief*. New York: Random House, 1990.

Lidell, Lucinda with Sara Thomas, Carola Beresford Cooke and Anthony Porter. *The Book of Massage: The Complete Step-by-Step Guide to Eastern and Western Techniques*. New York: Simon and Schuster, 1984.

Maanum, Armand with Herb Montgomery. *The Complete Book of Swedish Massage*. Minneapolis: Winston Press, 1985.

Maxwell-Hundson, Clare. *The Complete Book of Massage*. New York: Random House, 1988.

Rush, Anne Kent. *The Back Rub Book: How to Give and Receive Great Back Rubs*. New York: Random House, 1989.

Young, Jacqueline Young. *Self-Massage: The Complete 15-Minutes a Day Massage System for Health and Self-Awareness*. London: Thorsons, 1992.

Unseld-Baumanns, Christine. *Erotic Partner Massage*. New York: Sterling Publishing, 1990.

Sensual Massage

Inkeles, Gordon. *The New Sensual Massage: Learn to Give Pleasure with Your Hands*. New York: Bantam Books, 1992.

————. *Unwinding: Super Massage for Stress Control*. New York: Weidenfeld and Nicolson, 1988.

Lacroix, Nitya. *Sensual Massage: An Intimate and Practical Guide to the Art of Touch*. New York: Henry Holt, 1989.

Rush, Anne Kent. *Romantic Massage: Ten Unforgettable Massages for Special Occasions*. New York: Avon Books, 1991.

Russell, Stephen and Jurgen Kolb. *The Tao of Sexual Massage*. New York: Simon and Schuster, 1992.

Massage for Special Conditions

Ashley, Martin. *Massage: A Career at Your Fingertips*. New York: Station Hill Press,1992.

Dawes, Nigel and Fiona Harrold. *Massage Cures: The Family Guide to Caring and Curing Common Ailments with Simple Massage Techniques*. London: Thorsons, 1990.

Feltman, J. *Hands-on Healing: Massage Remedies for Hundreds of Health Problems*. Emmaus, Penn.: Rodale Press, 1989.

Jwing-Ming, Dr. Yang. *Chinese Qigong Massage: General Massage* . Jamaica Plain, Mass: Ymaa Publication Center, 1994.

Newton, Don. *Pathology for Massage Therapists.* Portland, Ore.: East-West College, Simran Publications, 1994.

Phaigh, Rich, and Perry Paul. *Athletic Massage*. New York: Simon and Schuster, 1984.

Thomas, Sara. *Massage for Common Ailments*. New York: Simon and Schuster, 1988.

Infants and Children

Auckett, Amelia D. *Baby Massage.* Melbourne, Australia: Hill of Content Publishing, 1981.

Chamberlain, David, Ph.D. *Babies Remember Birth and Other Extraordinary Scientific Discoveries about the Mind and the Personality of Your Newborn*. New York: Ballantine Books, 1988.

Cohen, Kenneth K., and Joan Hyme. *Imagine That!: A Child's Guide to Yoga*. Santa Barbara, Calif.: Santa Barbara Books, 1983.

Dass, Baba Hari. *A Child's Garden of Yoga*. Santa Cruz, Calif.: Sri Rama Publishing, 1980.

Goldsmith, Judith. *Childbirth Wisdom: From the World's Oldest Societies*. Brooklyn: East West Health Books, 1990.

Guyer, Evelyn A. *From the Hand to the Heart*. Elma, N.Y.: International Association of Infant Massage Instructors, 1992.

Leboyer, Frederick. *Loving Hands: The Traditional Indian Art of Baby Massage*. New York: Alfred A. Knopf, 1982.

Ludington-Hoe, Susan M., Ph.D. *Kangaroo Care: The Best You Can Do to Help Your Preterm Infant*. New York: Bantam Books, 1993.

Mcclure, Vimala Schneider. *Infant Massage: A Handbook for Loving Parents*. New York: Bantam Books, 1982.

Ramsey, Teresa Kirkpatrick, Bsn. *Baby's First Massage*. Centerville, Ohio: T.K. Ramsey, 1992.

Sinclair, Marybetts. *Massage for Healthier Children*. Oakland, Calif.: Wingbow Press, 1992.

Care Through Touch Institute

The **Care Through Touch Institute** is a state approved professional school of massage and pastoral ministry that offers training programs in the ministry of massage and the healing power of touch. CTI is recognized nationally and internationally for pioneering an embodied approach to pastoral ministry and Christian spirituality. Its courses provide sound training in the techniques of Massage: The Art of Anointing, in anatomy and physiology, in psychology and spirituality, in health education and business ethics. It sponsors a supervised pastoral internship program to assist students in adapting touch therapies and communication skills to the elderly, the ill and disadvantaged at field sites in the Oakland and San Francisco area. The heart and spiritual charter of **CTI** is the mission statement of Jesus, quoting the prophet Isaiah:

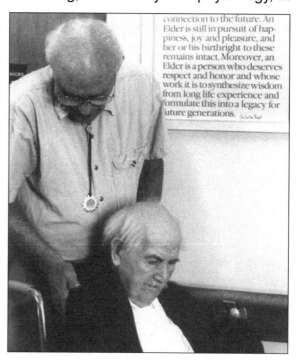

connection to the future. An Elder is still in pursuit of happiness, joy and pleasure, and her or his birthright to these remains intact. Moreover, an Elder is a person who deserves respect and honor and whose work it is to synthesize wisdom from long life experience and formulate this into a legacy for future generations.

The spirit of the Lord is upon me;
I have been anointed
to preach good news to the poor;
to proclaim freedom for the prisoners;
to release the oppressed;
to give sight to the blind.
—Jesus

The Institute's mission is to incarnate this same spiritual anointing in all of its training programs.

Mary Ann Finch, founder and director of the Care Through Touch Institute, is a teacher, body therapist and spiritual counselor.

Mary Ann has an M.A. in communications from Arizona State University and an M.A. in theology from the Graduate Theological Union in Berkeley, California.

She is a certified massage therapist and has studied health and humanistic psychology at Saybrook Institute in San Francisco. She has over thirty years of experience in eastern and western spirituality and a broad background in touch therapies and body awareness practices. She has trained and taught in healthcare clinics, hospitals and treatment centers throughout the United States, Europe and India.

Care Through Touch Institute
2401 LeConte Ave.
Berkeley, CA 94709